^{THE}SH*TFACED
GAMES

THE SH*TFACED GAMES

A SHOT AT GLORY AND GOLD FOR THE WASTED WARRIOR

HogWild

RUNNING PRESS
PHILADELPHIA · LONDON

Please drink responsibly. Never drink and drive. The author and publisher discaim all liability in connection with the use of this book.

Contents

**Mucho Importante Introduction
to Alcohol Awesomeness . . . 11**

Bronze-Medal Drinking Games . . . 16

GAME 1:
The Misty Hyman Butterfly Swim . . . 18

GAME 2:
The Get-Hammered Throw . . . 22

GAME 3:
**Drinking Bingo—
Synchronized Swimmers vs. Basketball Players . . . 24**

GAME 4:
Beer Relay Race . . . 28

GAME 5:
Eye-Candy Events . . . 30

SHITFACED COCKTAIL:
Shitfaced Nations of the World . . . 32

GAME 6:
Beer-Run Sprint . . . 34

GAME 7:
The Jerk and Clean . . . 36

GAME 8:
Shots Fired! . . . 38

GAME 9:
It's a Horse Race! . . . 39

GAME 10:

Giant Sloshed Slalom . . . 40

GAME 11:

Beer Bobsleigh . . . 43

SHITFACED COCKTAIL:

The Faceplant . . . 44

GAME 12:

Track and Field—Hurdles of Beer . . . 46

GAME 13:

Basketball Dunk . . . 48

GAME 14:

Snatch . . . 50

GAME 15:

Laughter Is the Best Medicine, and by Medicine, I Mean Beer . . . 52

SHITFACED COCKTAIL:

Sex on the Beach Volleyball . . . 54

GAME 16:

Beer Fencing . . . 56

GAME 17:

Beerathlon Brew-ski . . . 58

Silver-Medal Drinking Games . . . 60

GAME 18:

Who's on the Juice? . . . 62

GAME 19:

The Host with the Most (Alcohol) . . . 64

GAME 20:

I Put a Spell on You! . . . 66

GAME 21:

Ice-Rink Drink ... 68

SHITFACED COCKTAIL:

100-Meter Dash for the Border ... 70

GAME 22:

Make a Pass with Footsieball! ... 72

GAME 23:

Enunciate, Inebriate, Expectorate ... 75

GAME 24:

Make a Note of It! ... 78

SHITFACED COCKTAIL:

Miracle on Ice ... 80

GAME 25:

Act Out, Spazz Out ... 82

GAME 26:

Slap (Happy) Shots ... 84

GAME 27:

Alcohol Archery ... 86

GAME 28:

Volleybeer ... 88

GAME 29:

Pool Relay ... 89

GAME 30:

The Backstroke ... 90

GAME 31:

Ping-Pong Beer Bong ... 92

SHITFACED COCKTAIL:

Jessie Owens Beats the Nazis ... 94

GAME 32:

Wrestle for Beers . . . 96

GAME 33:

Shot Put Eggs Until You Vomelet! . . . 98

GAME 34:

Dice Hockey . . . 100

Gold-Medal Drinking Games . . . 102

GAME 35:

Tongues on Ice . . . 104

GAME 36:

Kissing the Medal . . . 106

GAME 37:

Sports Motion Sickness . . . 108

GAME 38:

I Figure You're Skating on Thin Ice! . . . 110

GAME 39:

Marathon Drinking . . . 112

GAME 40:

Dice Volleyball—Bump, Set, Spike the Punch! . . . 114

SHITFACED COCKTAIL:

A Shameful Johnson . . . 116

GAME 41:

Shots on Goal! . . . 118

GAME 42:

Skeet Shot . . . 120

GAME 43:

Snowboarding Tricks for Treats . . . 122

GAME 44:

The Drinking Triathlon . . . 125

SHITFACED COCKTAIL:

The Insane Usain . . . 126

GAME 45:

Basketball Fowl Shots . . . 128

GAME 46:

Dope Supplier . . . 130

SHITFACED COCKTAIL:

Swimming in Medals . . . 134

GAME 47:

Boxing Punch . . . 136

GAME 48:

Ski-Jump Crash and Burn . . . 140

SHITFACED COCKTAIL:

Spain Is Faking It . . . 142

GAME 49:

Don't Be a Loser—Guess the Winner! . . . 144

GAME 50:

Shot Put . . . Down Your Throat . . . 146

DRINKING QUIZ:

What Kind of Drunk Are You? . . . 150

Summer Olympic Games Host Cities . . . 156

Winter Olympic Games Host Cities . . . 157

Acknowledgments . . . 158

Mucho Importante Introduction to Alcohol Awesomeness

Welcome to the Shitfaced Games! World-class athletes train for their entire lives to have the chance to stand on the podium to be honored with a medal while their national anthem serenades their accomplishment.

Well, you will never be such an athlete. But you *can* compete at something you're good at: making an ass of yourself!

Yes! You've passed the trials, and now you've entered the Beer-athalon, the Drinking Events of the Shitfaced Games, and you just may enter the Alco-Hall of Fame!

NOTE TO UPTIGHT PEOPLE: Alcohol isn't all bad! In fact, scientists say wine has enzymes that make you look younger. I know this is true because when I drink three glasses of wine, everyone looks better.

One downside to alcohol is that there are so many liquor ads! Stop trying so hard, alcohol companies! I like you, but you're being clingy. We'll hook up this weekend, I promise!

Play it cool, beer and liquor corporations! I didn't forget about you—I've just been busy. I'll tell you what: I won't wait until midnight to be with you. I'll treat you right, and we'll get together over dinner and have the whole night together! You can even stay until morning and I'll take you out to brunch. I *do* care about this relationship, but you gotta stop bugging me so much when I'm watching my sports and twenty-one- to forty-nine-year-old demographic comedies!

My fellow drinkers, each game in this book has a medal signifying how Shitfaced it will get you.

Bronze:

You will get tipsy drunk.
Ex. After winning the Bronze I once told this girl that I loved her. I know—bad. And I didn't just tell her—I wrote it to her . . . in the snow with my pee.

Silver:

You will get slurred-speech drunky-doo.
Ex. After winning the Silver at a bar I once accidentally walked into the women's restroom. Of course, the girls were screaming. This one girl barked at me with attitude: "Can't you read?! The door has a big W!" I was like, "Yeah [hiccup] I thought it meant Welcome!"

Gold:

You will be falling-down drunk.
Ex. After winning the Gold
one night at the bar I shouted,
"I can't find my mouth!"
And it was true . . . because the tequila
I attempted to drink poured
straight onto my crotch.
It looked like I wet myself.
I guess I was literally "piss drunk."
Then I compounded my
stupidity when I
invited women to eat my
tequila worm.

DRINKING FACT: Alcohol affects every system in the body, including the skeletal system. That's why drunk people are more likely to bone. Aw! Ha ha!

Now get together with some friends to play the Shitfaced Games, and go for the Goldschläger!

When the USA wins Gold, I helped because I ate McDonald's and they sponsor the games. Sure, the athletes gave blood, sweat, and tears, but I'm the one risking a heart attack!

These drinking games are patterned after the world's most popular sports and athletic competitions. Some of these games are team events, and others will put you one-on-one against your drinking buddies. Please remember the spirit of the Games is not to win at all costs; it's to promote an atmosphere of cooperation so that you will help others get Shitfaced. You're a hero!

Besides drinking games, this book also includes seductive sports-themed cocktails and alarming facts.

Before beginning the games let's make sure we understand what it means to get "Shitfaced." As an example of Shitfacedness, I present to you a . . .

Classic Moment in Shitfaced History

My uncle enjoys a good sloshing, and I remember the last time he got Shitfaced. It was at the Thanksgiving dinner table.

Totally drunk and slurring his speech, he stood up to announce that he was going to tell all of us the "Story of Thanksgiving" and that the young ones at the table should pay special attention.

Here is what he said:

"Thanksgiving is a holiday when we give thanks to America's first president, Jesus Christ.

"President Jesus told the pilgrims to leave England and sail to the New World on a giant ship called Noah's Ark.

"The trip was very hard because the ship hit an iceberg and Leonardo DiCaprio drowned!

"In America the first thing the pilgrims built was Starbucks. But Starbucks did not serve coffee, only tea. The settlers protested and tossed all the tea in the river while dancing and having fun! That's why it was called the Boston Tea Party. The roof was set on fire and then raised. Somebody let the dogs out. And, reportedly, the shorties partied like it was their birthday.

"But there was an evil terrorist organization plotting to destroy the good pilgrim people. These terrorists were called turkeys.

"They were evil suicide turkeys because they would stuff themselves until they exploded, leaving a trail of destruction and dinner. It was delicious destruction!

"One turkey even kidnapped Jean-Claude Van Damme.

"I'm sorry, some of you college kids are too young to know who that is. One turkey even kidnapped SpongeBob SquarePants!

"But the pilgrims formed an alliance with the native people, and together they defeated this foul army of *eeeeeeevil* flightless birds.

"So the pilgrims invited the native people over to rejoice. Rejoice means to joice again. Which eventually became the state of New Joicey.

"All of this happened nearly four hundred . . . million years ago.

"In France Thanksgiving is called D-Day.

"So each year we give thanks to great pilgrims like Lewis and Clark, and Ben and Jerry. Oops, I'm sorry, I meant, *Tom* and Jerry.

"And now that we're done with our big meal, we conclude with the words of Dr. Martin Luther King Jr.: 'Free at last! Free at last! Thank God Almighty, the *bathroom* is free at last!'"

Yup, that was my Thanksgiving. Ya know, on Thanksgiving some families actually *play* football. I wish my family had that kind of coordination. Last year my dad got injured passing the salt.

BRONZE-MEDAL DRINKING GAMES

The Misty Hyman Butterfly Swim

A swimmer named Misty Hyman won the Gold medal in the two hundred–meter butterfly at the 2000 Summer Games.

Wow. Let's think of the ordeals she's had. These days everyone wants sympathy: Waaa, I have the fat gene. Waaa, I have asthma. Waaa, I can't afford an SUV. Waaa, my mom never made eye contact with me while breastfeeding and now I'm lactose intolerant!

At least your name isn't Misty Hyman! If your name ain't Misty Hyman, then you can't complain about a *damn thing*!

Think about Misty's childhood. Okay, usually the *kids* laugh at a funny name. But this name is so horrendous that even the *teachers* had to laugh while taking attendance. "Um, is Misty *Hyman* here? [*snicker snicker*] I'm looking for a Misty Hyman?" Some kid shouts out, "Aren't we all?!"

Where were the doctors on this? They should have stepped in here. The doc who delivered her parents' baby announced, "Congratulations, Mr. and Mrs. Hyman, it's a girl! What would you like to name her?"

"Um, we're thinking about Misty."

"Nooooooo!"

The doctor should have sat the parents down and had a heart-to-heart discussion. Something like: "Do you realize the long-term ramifications of this decision? Do you realize that your last name denotes a part of the female reproductive anatomy? Do you realize that the first name you've chosen, in conjunction with your last name, will give juvenile boys the giggles?"

So, no, you haven't gone through a damn thing. But Misty Hyman has! And she deserves her Gold medal.

Now you go earn your medal in this drinking game named in her honor.

How to Play

The butterfly swim stroke is one of the hardest strokes because it requires strength, stamina, and technique. This drinking game will also require strength of stomach, stamina to keep drinking, and careful technique so as not to spill. It's a team race against your opponents.

Divide everyone into teams of two. Each team will perform the contest while being timed by a stopwatch. At the end the team with the fastest time wins.

Drinker 1 wears two water wings full of beer and a snorkel mask.

NOTE FROM THE AUTHOR: Ya know, I can't swim. And I'm insecure about it. I tell people: "Hey! These are *not* water wings! They're not floaties!" I tell them very matter-of-factly: "These are *inflatable biceps!*" And then I strike the bodybuilder pose.

How do you fill water wings with beer? If you can't get it through the blow hole with a pressurized keg, then cut a hole in the water wing and create a flap, using duct tape to close the hole after filling it.

Drinker 1's teammate, Drinker 2, wears a Speedo.

Just kidding about the Speedo. Ya know, they say Speedos don't leave much to the imagination. Not true! I see a guy in Speedos and imagine gouging out my eyes with a lobster fork.

THE SH*TFACED GAMES

And random men in Speedos do not impress most women. Ladies prefer a polite man who isn't pointing at her.

Okay, start the timer!

Now Drinker 2 must position himself under his teammate's water wing biceps full of beer to squeeze out all the beer and drink it down.

After consuming all that beer Drinker 2 must fly around like a butterfly in a circle three times.

Then Drinker 2 must pour a shot of vodka down Drinker 1's snorkeling tube. If vodka spills to the floor, the team is disqualified. This is also known as a "Busted Hyman."

This is followed by two more shots of vodka poured down the snorkel tube. Then Drinker 1 must remove the snorkel and shout in a British accent: "Gold like Misty Hyman! There is absolutely nothing unfortunate about the name Misty Hyman!"

The Get-Hammered Throw

Just like the official Hammer Throw, in this game it's everyone for themselves.

How to Play

Soak a potato in vegetable oil until it is slippery. (To make this more challenging, use a large, irregularly shaped potato—you know, the kind that looks like your friend Bonk, the guy with a big head, wide ears, knot on his forehead, and three missing front teeth. And to think: that guy got more action than *you* last year! Tsk, tsk.)

Participants will be throwing the oiled potato, and the receiver must catch it with one hand. Furthermore, contestants may not wear a shirt (women and fat men with man hooters—or, as I call them, mooters—can wear bikini tops). And everyone must oil up their torso.

Use this opportunity to practice flexing and trash talking like your favorite professional wrestlers.

All the participants will now form a circle.

NOTE: **This is not a good time for you to encourage everyone to hold hands.**

The person holding the potato may throw it to anyone. The Hammer Throw is done at a 45-degree angle, and so is the Get-Hammered Throw. The person with possession of the oiled potato must throw underhanded, and the potato must arc in the air. In other words, no speed throws and no straight throws to the feet or legs.

GAME TIP: Toss the potato so it spins a lot to make it harder to catch!

You can throw the potato to anyone, even when they're not expecting it! Everyone must hold their beer in one hand while the other hand is used to catch the potato.

Inevitably some smart-ass will stretch out his loose jeans and catch the potato in his pants. If this happens, everyone is encouraged to jump on this person to make "mashed potatoes."

Anytime someone drops the potato he must chug his beer. If a contestant drops the potato three times, he is out.

Last one standing wins! And by standing, I mean swaying while desperately holding back a projectile puke storm! Yummy!

APOLOGY TO DUDES WITH MOOTERS: Guys, being chubby is okay, but you don't want random babies looking at your shirt and making suckling faces.

Drinking Bingo– Synchronized Swimmers vs. Basketball Players

Two teams battle for Bingo supremacy! That's right—Bingo. Bingo is an exciting game. It'll take your breath away! Why else do we always see Bingo players hooked up to oxygen tanks?

Ha ha, old people.

In Bingo there are those who are winners and those who have dozed off.

So we're gonna spice up our Bingo. And by spice up, I mean spiced rum!

NOTE: Rum can make anything better. Except forest fires. Don't spray fire with rum! It won't extinguish the flames; it will only make them dance and make out with each other!

How to Play

Team 1 is a synchronized swim team. Everyone must dress as a swimmer.

Guys, wear swimming trunks (a Speedo if you're daring or hilariously overweight) and no shirt. Girls, slip into your sexy swimsuit and sexiest shower cap.

NOTE: Guys, unless you are in some sort of Olympic competition, wearing Speedos will only win you the Gold medal in Too Much Information.

Team 2 is a basketball team. You must wear shorts, a basketball jersey, a sweatband around your head, and tattoos drawn in pen everywhere. High socks are a bonus.

Today's pro basketball players have gone too far with the tattoos. It's way too casual now to get a tattoo. I saw one guy with a tattoo on the back of his hand that said, "Milk, bread, eggs."

I guess his wife was pissed off that he kept forgetting to pick up those items at the grocery!

While drunk, I had the idea to get a tattoo of the word "truth" on my penis so I can say, "You can't handle the truth!" I hope she doesn't say, "Truth? Looks like a little white lie."

There will be five synchronized swimmers and five basketball players.

On the floor or ground draw a large Bingo card (five by five), making it big enough that a person can stand on each square, in chalk or masking tape (or with paint if you just don't give a hoot), and put Bingo numbers in each square. Make sure you mark the square in the middle as a free space.

The Bingo Caller will have access to a random number generator or an old-school Bingo machine.

NOTE: If you have an authentic Bingo machine, you are fucking rad! If you don't have one, you can easily get one by breaking into your local senior living facility.

When the number pops up, only the Bingo Caller sees it and then asks a trivia question that corresponds with the winning number. If a number pops up that is not on the board, pick another number.

For each question two players from opposing teams get ready to answer and run.

For example, if the randomly generated Bingo number is B-13, rather than announcing the number, the Bingo Caller may ask, "How many stripes are on the American flag?" Or "How many shots did Travis consume that night he committed a federal offense by puking in a mailbox?"

Players should run to the square that is marked 13.

If you get there first, you get the spot. If it's a tie, you do a shot with the other person. The first one to down their drink first wins the spot!

Whenever a synchronized swimmer wins a space he or she does a synchronized swimming motion. When a basketball player wins a space he takes an imaginary jump shot. If he forgets to do his move, he must drink.

If a player runs to the wrong spot, doesn't answer, or gets there too late, he has to take a drink and then stay on the sideline and wait for his turn to come up again.

The object for the players on your team is to form a Bingo line straight across any row, down any column, or diagonally. (A free-for-all sprint wins the free space, and the winner of the spot is whoever gets there and downs their shot first.)

When you win, the Bingo line becomes a drunken conga line as you dance while taunting your opponent!

The last time I was on a drunken conga line was at a family wedding. I felt a pair of hands on my waist, slipping down to my sculpted buns. *Those had better be a woman's hands!* I thought. They were—

a seventy-year-old woman's hands! I turned around while congaing (whoa, that's the first time I've ever used the word congaing! You just witnessed me losing my congaing virginity! There's the word congaing again! I can't help myself! I *like* it!), and I say to this near-octogenarian: "Excuse me, what do you think—are we related?" She answered, "I don't think so!"

So I look her over one more time. "Okay," I say, "well, if we *are* related, I'm sorry I don't remember you, but thanks again for the Bar Mitzvah gift. And if we're not related, let's make out under the limbo bar!"

She was game, and we bent over backward under the limbo bar. We kissed, and she called out, "Oh God!"

"Yeah, baby. I know I'm good! But don't attract any more attention—my parents wouldn't approve."

But she couldn't help herself and shouted again, "Oh *God!* My hip! It's broken again!"

Damn. It could have been a special night for me and Harriet.

Beer Relay Race

Everybody loves watching a good relay race. But just running? Really?

It would be more of a challenge for the track stars if metal spikes randomly shot up from the track or runners had to duck to avoid a dragon's tail slapping them in the head.

Ha, Dragon's Tail sounds like a fancy sushi roll. Why do they have to name sushi something fierce sounding? A dragon is big, strong, and breathes fires. Sushi is soft and kinda squishy. If anything, they should call it Dragon's Scrotum.

Although that would make it less appealing to order in the restaurant: "I'll have sashimi, a California roll, and the Dragon's, um, thingie."

Of course, the waiter will try to up-sell you: "Good choices! The Dragon's Scrotum goes very well with our special house Dragon Sake. Our chef brews it himself. It's a bit thicker and milkier, but it goes down smooth."

How to Play

Play this game on a track with four players to each team. Each player holds a closed can of beer. Each team has a different lane, and the players on each team stand at different spots on their track.

Before you can hand off your beer can, you must completely empty its contents by ingesting the beer. You can either chug the beer and then run, drink while running, or run then chug. To prove you have emptied your beer can, you must turn your can upside down over the next runner's head before he or she may begin running.

At this point the next runner may crack open his can of beer or begin running. The first team to cross the finish line is the winner! Of course, Player 4 may not cross the finish line until he has consumed his beer.

When you win let out a victorious *burrrrrrrrrp!*

Ew, it smells like Dragon Sake! Aw! Ha ha!

NOTE: Back when I was a teacher, a nine-year-old said to me: "Grown-ups can drink—*why can't I?*!!!" Because you're yelling, demanding attention, and unwilling to listen to reason. It's like you're already drunk!

Eye-Candy Events

Swimming and volleyball are the eye-candy events of international competitions. So this drinking event will focus on eyes and candy!

To that end, competitive swimming is unfair! Women, you get to see wet, naked men with muscles and a six-pack. But the female swimmers are flat-chested with big arms, wearing an ugly one-piece and granny's shower cap.

How to Play

This is a one-on-one drinking game. If you blink, you lose and must take a shot of liquor.

Player 1 has two minutes to make Player 2 blink her eyes by using candy in any way he wants, except he can't touch the other player.

For instance, you may want to make the other player blink through laughter as you slowly and seductively deep-throat a thick chocolate bar. Or maybe you will use the chocolate bar as a ridiculous mustache and start talking like a professor.

Or perhaps you will act out a dramatic love scene with Gummi Bears humping.

You can try to make your opponent blink by throwing the candy, juggling it, or doing something so absurd that she blinks her eyes in disbelief!

You can do whatever you like with the candy to make your

opponent blink. After the two-minute round it's her turn to make you blink.

What would make *me* blink is if she arranged her Skittles into the shape of a heart. And by heart, I mean boobies! And by boobies, I mean a brain. Because I have no interest in the female form, only in soft, squishy, squeezy brain matter. Yes, sexy, sexy synapses!

SH*TFACED
COCKTAIL

Shitfaced Nations
of the World

Eight nations are represented in this drink symbolizing the Shitfaced Games creed of cultural diversity, open-mindedness, and cirrhosis of the liver.

2 ounces Kraken dark rum (for the USA)

1 splash Coke

1 splash Magners Irish Cider (for Ireland)

1 ounce Stoli vodka (for Russia)

1/2 ounce tequila (for Mexico)

1 ounce Beefeater gin (for England)

2 ounces triple sec (for France)

1/2 ounce ice cold Jäger (for Germany)

1/2 ounce sake, preferably the sweet kind with a low "san-do" (for Japan)

5 ounces sweet-and-sour mix

lemon slice

Stir all the ingredients well and serve cold over ice. After consuming this drink you'll be feeling peaceful, singing, "We Are the World," but your off-key crooning will cause nearby people of all nationalities to threaten you with violence until you plead, "Can't we all just get along?!" Let's learn from the alcohol! Then you preach, "Let's speed up that day when all of God's liquors, dark rums and light rums, kosher wines and unkosher, apéritifs and digestifs, will be able to join in our stomachs and sing!"

NOTE TO MEN ALL OVER THE WORLD: If you drink too much, your romance rod might fail to function properly. Women prefer a penis that looks like a Roman solider with great posture, not one that looks like a beggar in a raincoat with slumped shoulders.

Beer-Run Sprint

It's time to make a beer run!

How to Play

Alcohol Athlete 1 holds a full cup of beer in each hand and runs to his teammate, who is waiting for his beers. If the runner spills any beer on the ground or floor (it helps to have a referee), he must stop immediately and chug one beer.

I suggest using a normal cup of beer and not the big stein they give you at Oktoberfest.

NOTE: In Germany everything is big: the beer, the pretzels, and the aspirations for global domination.

Then he continues the run.

After the hand-off Alcohol Athlete 2 runs to hand off to Alcohol Athlete 3, who runs toward the finish line!

This game can, of course, work with more or less runners so long as each team has the same number of Alcohol Athletes.

All members of the losing teams must chug a beer to prepare for the re-match!

For an extra challenge, don't let anyone use the bathroom. The running will get funnier as people are doing the pee-pee dance!

I wonder why the pee-pee dance works. I think there's a simple scientific explanation: when you shift your weight back and forth, the urine held in your bladder does not permit itself to be discharged from the urethra because it says, "Oh, it's been so long since I've been dancing! This is fun! Finally, a chance to shake my groove thang! I'm not leaving!"

The Jerk and Clean

The clean and jerk is a weightlifting competition. In college I once came back home to catch my dorm mate practicing this event. He was watching instructional videos on the Internet. Awww! Ha ha!

In this drinking game version you will be doing the Jerk and Clean in a race against your competitors.

How to Play

Each team has a player who will jerk and clean while his or her teammate will attempt to swallow beer.

Player 1 gets on his knees, ready to receive a nice head of beer. Referees oversee the action and shout, "On your mark, get set, jerk!"

Player 2 then jerks a closed can of beer ten times and pours it down into the mouth of Player 1 as fast as possible to win the race.

The winning team will be first to finish the entire beer *and* have a clean face with no beer on it. So jerk quickly, swallow fast, then clean your face!!

NOTE: I once saw a guy, after winning a weightlifting competition, actually bend down to kiss the weights. Man, if that guy is so affectionate with his weights, imagine what he does with his Nautilus Machine!

Shots Fired!

There are many shooting games involving rifles and handguns. But I'm not gonna have you shoot while drinking! Because if there's one thing this book is about, it's personal safety.

So you can't shoot while wasted, but you will get the next best thing to shooting: the *sound* of shots fired!

How to Play

Begin by stretching to get your body limber for this athletic event. And by stretching, I mean stretching your throat open to chug a beer.

Each team gets an equally sized, large sheet of bubble wrap—the bigger the better.

The entire team helps to pop every single bubble. The first team to announce they have finished wins! But if the other team can find even one bubble that the first team missed, Team 1 is disqualified and Team 2 wins instead.

Every member of the losing team must drink a shot.

Play multiple rounds!

And remember, stay safe while drinking and safe while sha-boinking. In fact, put bubble wrap over your fun parts. That way when you're having sex, it'll sound like you're making popcorn!

It's a Horse Race!

There are many beautiful horse races and presentation events to honor the world's greatest equestrian athletes. Think of the proud, refined history and art of horse riding as you proceed to act like a horse's ass.

How to Play

Each team has one player down on all fours as the horse, with a second player riding on top of him as the jockey. The jockey must hold a can of beer while riding.

If the jockey falls off the horse, the horse must immediately stop and wait for the jockey to remount.

The first team to cross the finish line is the winner. The losers must neigh like angry horses and chug a beer.

Ya know, being a jockey isn't easy. Consider how difficult it is for him to find a beautiful and intelligent maiden to marry. He's barely five feet tall, and his career is spent staring at the rear end of the horse in front of him. Poor guy. Maybe that's why jockeys are known to have quick, angry tempers. I knew a jockey who was hot headed yet cold as ice. He disappeared in a cloud of condensation.

Giant Sloshed Slalom

Snowboarding giant slalom is a race against competitors down the mountain between the poles.

WINTER GAMES FACTOID: Organizers of the 2010 Winter Games were upset when snowboarders used the Olympic Torch to light up a joint.

This drinking game version calls for a flat, paved, open space such as a parking lot, empty street, or basketball court.

NOTE TO IDIOTS: Do not play drinking games on a flat, paved space that happens to be the roof of a building. Drinking and falling off a building is so cliché. It's okay to be a drunk a-hole, but don't be an unoriginal a-hole!

NOTE TO SELF: Why did I just say "a-hole" when, clearly, anybody who has purchased this book will not be offended if I use a naughty word to reference the colon's exhaust pipe?

How to Play

Two or more teams must race to be the first team to cross the finish line. Each team will have two participants.

Player 1 sits on a skateboard representing the snowboard. Player 2 pushes Player 1 to the finish line.

Player 1, while sitting on the skateboard, must hold a beer and completely finish it before crossing the finish line. The only place you may pour the beer is down your throat. You may only consume the beer while the skateboard is in motion. The speed you go is up to you.

If Player 1 falls off the skateboard, the team loses.

Remember: before crossing the finish line you must finish the beer or you are disqualified. The losing team chugs beers.

For an extra challenge create a course with flags just like the snowboard giant slalom that requires the teams to make turns. Or have the teams race around in a square shape from start to finish while staying inside the flags.

For extra fun, if you live in a cold winter climate, make the losing team perform fellatio on a snowman's green pickle dick.

CONSERVATION NOTE: **After you eat the pickles, don't discard the juice in the jar! Freeze it to create pickle popsicles! Give them to all the kids who aggravate you!**

Beer Bobsleigh

Bobsleigh is the winter sport in which two men lay down to squeeze themselves romantically together into a giant penis.

How to Play

Make two or more ramps by using a half-pipe of PVC or something similar and nontoxic. You can also use a large, flat tray, a large basin, or a bath tub. Fill the half-open piping with beautiful beer. Tape a paper flag to a toothpick and stick it into a marshmallow—now your marshmallow has a sail. Float the marshmallow in the beer.

Teammate 1 blows the marshmallow down the beer-filled piping or tray full of beer. It's extra cool if the piping goes around corners.

Teammate 2 needs to capture the marshmallow toboggan in his or her mouth. He should swallow the marshmallow—taking out the toothpick, of course. The first team to swallow their beer-soaked marshmallow wins!

If you've ever dipped marshmallows into beer before, you might be an alcoholic. Alcoholism is the only disease where you can be in denial. You never see someone with heart disease yell, "I can stop having atherosclerosis whenever I want!"

SH*TFACED COCKTAIL

The Faceplant

Drink this, and you'll feel like a gymnast
who lands on her face!
You'll be guaranteed to fall off any balance beam!

Split the glass (get it? Split? Ha!) with:

$3/4$ ounce Jim "Balance" Beam

2 gymnastic rings of pineapple

2 dashes lemon-lime soda

$3/4$ ounce rum

$3/4$ ounce vodka

1 gymnast "wedgie" of mango

Mix all the ingredients well by spinning the glass like a gymnast, then serve over ice. Now try to stick the landing!

Dear gymnasts,

You could be doing those handstands over a beer keg! Oh, all that talent wasted on not getting wasted!

Sincerely drunk,
HogWild

Track and Field– Hurdles of Beer

Are you aware that many of the world's top track stars ice their nipples before a race to get a slight advantage? Okay, I made that up, but it would be awesome to hear the TV announcer shout, " . . . and Johnson wins by a nipple!"

How to Play

Set up a track with beers in each lane. There should be four beers per lane, each about forty-five feet from each other. You must run to the beer, chug it completely, and then show the judges you have finished it by turning the can upside down over your head.

If you have failed to chug the beer completely, you are disqualified. Once you have chugged your beer, dash to the next beer. The first athlete to chug the final beer and cross the finish line is the winner!

For extra drinking fun each athlete should represent a different nation by wearing an appropriate shirt and downing a relevant beer. So Patricia can wear a green "Kiss Me, I'm Irish" shirt while chugging Guinnesses, and Pearl sports her "Jamaican Me Crazy" shirt while guzzling Red Stripes!

Now run like the wind! A fart can be like a turbo boost from your butt!

That reminds me: my ex-girlfriend used to tell me to hurry up and get my ass in gear. Then I'd fart. She would yell at me in disapproval, so I'd answer, "Hey, if you want me to get my ass in gear, you gotta be okay with the sound of the engine!"

Basketball Dunk

I love basketball. I grew up in the Bronx playing on street basketball courts, and the game taught me about earning respect and standing up for myself. The guys would call me names like Wonder Bread because I was the only white kid out there.

Now, I could have cried or threatened violence, but instead, I didn't let the guys get to me—I just played basketball. I was a tough rebounder. I made some jump shots and missed some jump shots. I drove to the hoop. I wouldn't back down.

And over time the guys stopped calling me Wonder Bread but would say, "Hey, good game, Kiki Vandeweghe!" See, at the time, Kiki Vandeweghe was a white guy of average ability who played for the Knicks. Yes, I *earned* the right to be called . . . Kiki.

How to Play

Pour a can of beer into a large salad bowl or something similar.

The game's moderator is charged with the duty of obtaining lots of fairly easy trivia questions. These can be questions about sports, each other, or general knowledge.

Then, each player is asked an easy question. If a player gets it right, he survives the round. If he gets it wrong, the moderator dunks his head into the bowl of beer, then holds his head in the bowl (but with his nose out so he can breathe!).

The player is not allowed to remove his face from the bowl until he slurps up all the beer. If he raises his hand to give up before consuming all the beer, he's out of the game.

The last player remaining is the best baller!

Did I ever tell you about the time I caught my college roommate palming his balls? When I walked in he was so startled that he double dribbled all over his midcourt!

Now guys, you'll probably get ideas while you're practicing your lonely lay-ups in front of your computer and web cam. If you're thinking, "Is it OK to send a random girl a picture of my penis?" The answer is yes, but first you must send her two photos of dinners at nice restaurants.

Snatch

In this simple drinking game named for weightlifting's snatch competition, two teams each send a player to face off against his opposition to prove he is stronger than a cute little kitty's desire to take a nap curled up on the couch, bathed in warm sunshine gleaming through the window. Damn, I love naps. They're like the mini-donuts of sleep.

How to Play

Two opponents grasp one very cold, slippery, wet can of beer, holding the can horizontally and wrapping their hands around either the left or right half of the beer can. The referee will shout, "On your mark, get set, *snatch!*"

The winner is the competitor who successfully snatches the beer for himself out of his opponent's hand.

If the beer falls to the ground, scramble to snatch it up!

No hitting or activity of any kind is allowed except the one hand wrapped around the beer.

The loser must stick his face near the can of beer, and the winner then shakes it and opens it, squirting the loser with the snatch. Then the loser must chug the beer!

After I chug a few beers I'm really good with girls. For instance, I knew this girl liked me because, as I talked to her, she kept looking at her watch! That's right, baby, time flies when you're having fun!

Laughter Is the Best Medicine, and by Medicine, I Mean Beer

You know what sport makes me laugh? Curling.

You know—that funny-looking ice sport with the brooms? Men and women alike compete in this highly ridiculous event.

So this drinking game isn't about curling but about laughing!

How to Play

Pair off against your opponent. Player 1 must make Player 2 smile or laugh within two minutes using any means necessary except touching. Player 2 must watch and listen to Player 1 all while holding a mouthful of beer.

Player 1 earns:

ONE POINT for making his opponent smile

TWO POINTS for making his opponent laugh

THREE POINTS for making his opponent laugh so hard she spits her beer

ONE HUNDRED POINTS for making his opponent spit her beer through her nose!

After each two-minute round the player with the most points is the winner. The player with the least points must chug a beer. Agree on the number of rounds beforehand, and make 'em laugh!

NOTE: Making people laugh should be easier in the later rounds after they've laughed and chugged the comedy club–style two-drink minimum.

Suggestions on how to make your opponent laugh:

- Tell a funny joke.
- Hold up a mirror so she can see how silly she looks with her cheeks full of beer. Then shout, "You look like a squirrel on a beer run for his buddies!"

SH*TFACED COCKTAIL

Sex on the
Beach Volleyball

1 ounce vodka

$^1/_2$ ounce peach schnapps

8 ounces orange juice

1 dash grenadine

1 ounce coconut rum

$^1/_2$ ounce vanilla vodka

$^1/_2$ ounce tequila

a little bit of sugar

Pour the vodka and the peach schnapps into a glass over ice. Fill the rest with the orange juice and add the dash of grenadine.

That's a Sex on the Beach. Now let's add the volleyball part.

"Bump" up the alcohol content with 1 ounce of coconut rum.

"Set" yourself up a fun night with $^1/_2$ ounce of vanilla-flavored vodka.

"Spike" it with $^1/_2$ ounce of tequila.

Mix it up and pour into a glass that you have filled with $^1/_8$ inch of beautiful white sand in the form of sugar.

Yes, the Olympics are sexy: men watching volleyball, women watching swimmers, and gay men and women watching weightlifters.

Beer Fencing

Fencing is an exhilarating competition in which two combatants use a long blade called a foil. In this sport you thrust your weapon into your opponent's torso, neck, or groin.

SAFETY NOTE: **Never thrust your love weapon into an untrusted target groin. It's better to practice fencing by yourself. Gals and guys, don't think of it as masturbation. Think of it as a congratulatory handshake for staying out of trouble.**

How to Play

Two players face off wearing roller skates or, if you don't have roller skates, go barefoot on a slippery oiled-up or soapy floor, wear socks on a polished wood floor, or wear normal shoes while being very, very drunk. Strap on a helmet and pads!

Fence each other with Nerf swords, broom handles, Wiffle ball bats, or something that's fun yet won't cause stab wounds. (I learned that after feedback from this book's first edition, when I recommended using adult walrus tusks.)

NOTE: **No walruses were harmed in the writing of that joke. They were wisdom tusks and had to be pulled anyway.**

One hand holds your fencing stick while the other holds your beer. The first person to spill their beer is the loser and must chug the rest of it!

IMPORTANT ANIMAL CONSERVATION FACT: Each year thousands of child walruses are injured while sleeping because they've placed their baby tusks under their pillow for the tooth fairy.

Beerathlon Brew-ski

The biathlon is cross-country skiing combined with shooting targets. It's a very natural fit, just like dunking cookies in concrete mix.

How to Play

Participants are timed as they complete the Beerathlon course. The winner is the Beerathlete with the fastest time!

This game is best played wearing socks on a slick wood floor (or other slippery surface) as you slide across in the style of cross-country skiing.

Set up open trash bins as the targets and, with lines of chalk or masking tape, create a course. The targets/bins should be a decent distance away from the course so shooting the target is a challenge.

As you slide across the floor you will be holding a can of beer in each hand. These are your ski poles.

Cross-country ski across the floor as fast as you can to the first spot marked with an *X*. Then chug one beer as quickly as possible and then shoot the empty can into the target.

If you miss the target, as a penalty, fifteen seconds are added to your final time.

IDIOTIC IDEA: In the real biathlon it'd be cool if they lined up, like, fifty snowmen, and the athletes had to shoot Frosty's head straight off his fat, snowy body!

After shooting at the beerathlon target your beverage is replaced with a new can. Now ski to the second spot and chug your beer. Shoot the target. Then brew-ski to the third and final target to chug and shoot.

Your final course time is recorded, and any penalties from missing the targets are added.

The winner celebrates by making everyone else chug an extra beer for losing. That means everyone will chug at least three beers in this game, with the losers chugging a fourth beer that tastes like shame.

SHAMEFUL BIATHLON FACT: Russian biathlete Olga Pyleva was thrown out of the Olympics and stripped of her Silver medal for failing a drug test. I reviewed her photo from back then, and I think the beautiful Olga Pyleva should be forgiven.

NOTE: By "reviewed her photo," I meant I ogled Olga. I ogled Olga's old Olympic photo! Oy!

DRINKING FACT: Just two drinks can decrease coordination for eighteen hours. Recite this fact when apologizing for making love like a scared flamingo.

SILVER-MEDAL DRINKING GAMES

Who's on the Juice?

International sports have strict drug testing to prevent athletes from "juicing" to gain an advantage. And in this Shitfaced drinking game alcohol athletes will try to guess who is consuming all-natural spirits and who is on "the juice."

Juicing is a real problem in sports. A number of athletes have been famously stripped of their medals after they were found to have been secretly sprouting a beautiful horse tail.

Even female gymnast Kjerti Romanski was accused of being on the juice! Kjerti Romanski!

AUTHOR'S NOTE: All the athletes mentioned in this book are real—except Kjerti Romanski. I made up that name because I thought it sounded gymnastical.

AUTHOR'S SECOND NOTE: I also made up the word gymnastical because I like it.

How to Play

The scorekeeper hands out slips of paper informing each competitor whether he will be playing this round Natural or Juicing, meaning he will be getting either a cup of alcohol or juice.

The scorekeeper will fill opaque cups with either a screwdriver (vodka and orange juice) or just plain orange juice.

The first contestant drinks the contents of his cup, trying to trick everyone into believing he is drinking the *opposite* of what he has.

So if the player is drinking a strong screwdriver, he will try to make it seem like it's regular orange juice, and if drinking orange juice, the player will try to convince the other players that it's a screwdriver.

The other participants write down whether they think the drinking player is Natural or on the Juice. They hand their answers to the scorekeeper.

IMPORTANT NOTE: Before the game begins, each player does a shot of vodka while everyone else watches so they can see each other's "vodka face." This will help players judge if other participants are Natural or Juicing once the game begins. Each player then does one more pregame shot. This is to help players achieve ancient yoga's fourth meditative stage called Dhyana, or more commonly known as, "Duuuuuuuude! I love you, man!"

Scoring:

Nondrinking players get ten points for a correct guess.

The drinking player gets ten points for each participant he fools.

Now it is the next person's turn to drink and try to fool everyone.

The winner is announced after three rounds of drinking.

But really, everyone's a winner in terms of their vitamin C intake.

Drunken Thought: **Alcohol causes me to say stupid things such as this:**

Her: **You're very well read!**

Me: **That's because I spend a lot of time on the toilet. This is the best first date ever!**

The Host with the Most (Alcohol)

Just how well do you know the nations of the world? Can you tell Ecuador apart from Eritrea? And can you do it when you're so drunk that you can't tell your ass from your elbow? I was once so drunk I couldn't tell my ass from my elbow. That's why I said to the girl in my bed: "Damn, I look good!" Then before I made sweet sha-boinking to her, I got frisky and slapped my own elbow.

How to Play

A referee will consult the lists of Olympic host cities at the back of this book on pages 156–157 and challenge each player to name the city's country within three seconds or else the player must drink.

Answer correctly and stay in the game. Give three wrong answers and you're out.

If you answer incorrectly and the right answer is a North American country, drink a shot of beer.

If you're wrong and the correct answer is a European country, drink a shot of vodka.

If your answer was mistaken and the correct answer is an Asian country, drink a shot of sake or an Asian beer like Sapporo or Tsingtao.

For example, if the moderator of the game announces, "The 1896 Summer Games was held in Athens," and it's your turn, you have three seconds to shout out the country "Greece" or you must drink a shot of vodka.

"The 1920 Summer Games were in Antwerp." You must shout out "Belgium" within three seconds or drink a shot of vodka.

"The 1960 Winter Games were held in Squaw Valley." If you don't answer "the United States," you must do a shot of beer.

The last geographically intelligent drinker remaining is the winner!

Hey, it's not easy to be smart when you're tipsy! When I'm drunk I say stupid things, like one time I said, "Summer's Eve is a dumb name! I'm going to invent a better product called Winter's Eve!" Then I put on my best commercial announcer voice for the slogan: "Winter's Eve Douche gives your hoo-ha a fresh wintergreen scent like a snowy pine tree."

Then my date looked at me quizzically and left the restaurant.

Have a blast with this game, and laugh at your friends' geography ignorance!

NOTE: I still remember the names of the Great Lakes because of the mnemonic HOMES. Now if only they came up with a mnemonic device to help me remember the spelling of mnemonic! Whoever invented that spelling is a mnincompoop!

I Put a Spell on You!

This is a great game to play after Game 19 because in this challenge two teams battle by spelling the names of Olympic host cities. Use the city lists at the back of this book on pages 156–157.

How to Play

Team 1 picks an Olympic year (hopefully it will have a difficult-to-spell host city). The referee announces the name of the host city. Players on Team 2 get together to figure it out and then must spell the name of that city.

If Team 2 spells the city incorrectly, everyone on the team must take a shot. If Team 2 spells the city correctly, everyone on Team 1 must take a shot.

If the referee informs Team 1 that they have chosen a year that did *not* host an Olympics, then everyone on Team 1 must drink.

The first team forced to drink three shots is the loser.

Example:

Team 1 chooses 1994. The moderator tells Team 2 they must spell Lillehammer.

Because Team 2 is hammered, they misspell it as *Lilyhammer*. Now they must all take a shot.

Now Team 2 chooses 1952. The moderator tells Team 1 that they must spell Helsinki. Team 1 spells it correctly. So now Team 2 must drink again. One more drink will be their third shot, causing them to lose.

Ya know, a drinking game is the rare game that's actually fun to lose. It's kinda like playing strip poker when you're an exhibitionist!

Ice-Rink Drink

It's Shitfaced hockey, baby! So prepare to black out . . . your front teeth!

How to Play

In this hockey game a coin is the puck. For readers in the near future, a coin is a form of currency used in ancient times before the existence of credit cards and electronic banking. It was a powerful little piece of metal that allowed people to do laundry, get a handful of M&M's, and park for multiple minutes on a city street, and sometimes it was used to assist in making important decisions such as whether or not to invade Poland.

Each team sets up their side of the table by positioning, any way they want, three bottles of alcohol as their hockey defensemen, except only one may go in between the goal posts. Goal posts can simply be two cans of beer.

For example, you may put a bottle of whiskey in between the goal posts, a can of beer on the left side of the table, and a bottle of vodka on the middle-right side of the table.

The point of the game is to shoot the puck (by flicking a coin with your thumb) into the other team's goal. Each team gets three flicks of the puck (coin) to try for the opposing team's goal. If a team has more than one member, players take turns shooting the puck.

Each time the puck hits your opposing team's bottle of alcohol, each player on your team must do a shot of that bottle's contents.

Each time your team scores a goal, each member of the opposing team must take a shot of the alcohol with the highest proof on their side of the table.

NOTE: If that alcohol is anything ending with the word "spritzer" or "lemonade," the entire team must submit to a hockey check to their passion area to verify the existence of adult genitalia.

If the opposing team does not score a goal, start with the puck in its current position.

The winner is the first team to score three goals.

Because Russians, Swedes, Canadians, Americans, Czechs, and Finns (Finlandians? Finnishers? Finlanders? Nah, let's go with Helsinki-raisers!) dominate ice hockey, only alcohol from these nations is acceptable: American spirits such as Jack Daniels or Jim Beam, Canadian whiskey such as Crown Royal, Canadian beers, Czech beers, Russian vodka such as Stoli, Swedish vodka like Absolut, and Finnish vodka such as Finlandia.

Finlandia is a funny name for a vodka. There should be a vodka called Americandia. Or from the state it comes from, like Idaho-ly Shit I'm Fucked Up.

Vodka has funny names. I'd make a vodka and name it aptly, such as: Putin's Waterbottle, SmirPuke, Grey Guts, or Hangoverinchki.

SH*TFACED COCKTAIL

100-Meter Dash
for the Border

Mexico was the first Latin American country to host the Olympics! Let's celebrate with a dash for the border!

½ ounce limeade concentrate (about ⅛ can)

Fire a shot from the starter's pistol by pouring in 1 shot of gold tequila

Aw, what the hell, fire another shot . . . of tequila!

(For those measuring strictly, this should equal about 2 ounces total, or ¼ cup.)

6 ounces Mexican beer (about ½ can)

lime wedge

dash of Mexican hot sauce

Stir all of the ingredients and pour into an 8-ounce glass over ice.

This drink will have you feeling frisky, so make sure you use a rubber sombrero!

FACTOID: Did you know the official colors of Mexico are red and green? They symbolize salsa and guacamole.

NOTE: Factoids do not have to contain facts.

Make a Pass with Footsieball!

Football (aka soccer) features great passes. And now it's your chance to make a pass!

NOTE: **Usually female soccer players are fit and cute! But not so at my college. Our girls' soccer team was nicknamed the Stampede.**

How to Play

Play with up to thirteen people, and everyone is assigned a number ranging from 1 through 13.

When it's your turn pick a card from a playing deck until someone's number is drawn—ace is 1, jack is 11, queen is 12, and king is 13. Make a pass at that person, and make it believable! Use your best pick-up line, flirt with your eyes, touch their hand, play footsie, bust out your moves!

NOTE: **Ladies, when I'm super old, I'll still be naughty. I'll play footsies under the table with my thick sneakers until our Velcro gets all tangled!**

If the person wants to turn down your pass, he must be out of his mind, because you're hawt! Nevertheless, drink a shot.

If he accepts your pass, now *you* can back down from your original advance, but then you must drink a shot.

If this girl or guy accepts your pass and you also accept, you two will kiss on the lips. As you kiss, everyone else puts on their best excited soccer announcer voice to yell, "Gooooooooooooooooal!" For some it will be a game of chicken to dare the other person! After everyone has taken three turns, the winner is the player who has had the least number of shots, or in other words, has accepted the most kisses.

Everyone who loses must now take an extra shot, which, coincidentally, will make them more likely to kiss someone!

Just don't fall in love! Because love is like NASCAR. Sometimes you feel like you're going around in circles until you become a total wreck that your friends need to pull you out of.

Enunciate, Inebriate, Expectorate

One of the greatest moments in sports history was when the 1980 American team of amateur hockey players overtook the commie Soviet team of professionals who had won almost every Olympic tournament and world championship for the past twenty-six years.

Celebrate this by attempting to pronounce the names of the players while being all slurry drunk-like.

How to Play

Obtain a deck of cards. If you don't have one available, you can easily get them by breaking and entering into any senior living facility, especially the one where you got that old-school Bingo machine (page 25)! Those places don't have any serious security. But I'm sure your grandma is safe . . . not that you'd know, as you haven't called her. Ah, whatever. She can fend for herself. She can probably kick some serious ass with those chunky diabetic shoes.

Shuffle the cards. Choose a card. If it's a red card, you have to pronounce the next commie name on the list. Choose a black card and you must pronounce the next American name on the list. The list is at the end of this game.

If you mess up the pronunciation, then you must take a shot. Screw up the Soviet name and take a shot of vodka; mess up the American name and take a shot of domestic beer.

This is not that easy considering that while drunk you will be attempting to quickly pronounce names that include Vladislav Tretiak, Viacheslav Fetisov, and Aleksandr Skvortsov. You'll breathe a sigh of relief when it's time to say Bill Baker!

NOTE: That is, unless you are Russian and reading the translation of this book, in which case you'll shout, "Damn you, Bill Baker, and your crazy name!"

Depending on the number of players, decide how many screw-ups will cause you to lose.

Ya know, hockey would be more interesting if some of the players were drinking heavily.

Hockey Fan 1: Wow! Look at Checkoffskis! He's unpredictable out there! You think he's going to skate left, then he suddenly goes right!

Hockey Fan 2: Um, I don't think he's faking out the defense. I think he's stumbling around drunk.

Hockey Fan 1: Whatever! It's great!

Hockey Fan 2: Uh-oh. I think he just threw up in his helmet.

Now if you've learned anything from this game, it's that you need to call your grandma! Also, senior living facilities are great places to go "shopping" for backgammon sets and televisions.

NOTE: Just kidding! Don't go to old-age homes to steal their stuff! Go there to keep them company and steal their hearts. Then steal their pensions.

Russian Players

Vladislav Tretiak
Viacheslav Fetisov
Alexei Kasatonov
Vladimir Petrov
Valeri Kharlamov
Boris Mikhailov
Helmuts Balderis
Zinetula Bilyaletdinov
Aleksandr Golikov
Vladimir Golikov
Vladimir Krutov
Yuri Lebedev
Sergei Makarov
Aleksandr Maltsev
Vladimir Myshkin
Vasili Pervukhin
Aleksandr Skvortsov
Sergei Starikov
Valeri Vasiliev
Viktor Zhluktov

American Players

Jim Craig
Ken Morrow
Mike Ramsey
Mark Johnson
Rob McClanahan
Dave Silk
Bill Baker
Neal Broten
Dave Christian
Steve Christoff
Mike Eruzione
John Harrington
Steve Janaszak
Jack O'Callahan
Mark Pavelich
Buzz Schneider
Eric Strobel
Bob Suter
Phil Verchota
Mark Wells

Make a Note of It!

In this game you will be drunk and guessing what's written on your forehead. Except this time you won't have to look in the mirror as you desperately try to clean off magic marker from the night before!

How to Play

The moderator of this game takes a bunch of sticky notes and writes an Olympic sporting event on each one. Everyone takes a note and, without looking at them, sticks them on their foreheads.

NOTE: If you don't have sticky notes, you can also use small pieces of paper and a piece of chewed gum to smush the note to your forehead.

NOTE TO ENGLISH SPEAKERS: Did you know that some dictionaries don't consider *smush* to be an officially recognized word? C'mon, dictionary gatekeepers! If *bling* is a word, certainly *smush* can be a word! It's a beautiful amalgam of squish and mush!

Everyone sits in a circle with the sporting event written on their forehead for all to read.

To discover what it says on your head, you may ask someone a question—for example: "Am I a winter or summer sport?"

If you can't guess the right answer, then you must drink. Then it's the next player's turn. Each player may ask up to four questions.

If the person answering you gives an incorrect answer, as determined by the rest of the group, *he* must chug everything in his cup.

The first person to name the sport on their forehead correctly wins the Gold medal, second place wins Silver, and third place wins Bronze.

Everyone who does not earn a medal must drink one last time to drown their shame.

You know what I've realized? The Olympics are like a sexy ex who comes back in your life years later and you get excited. But after one week you remember why you stopped caring about her.

And that's why we drink!

SH*TFACED COCKTAIL

Miracle on Ice

Miracle on Ice is the name given to the 1980 miracle victory of American amateur hockey players over the greatly favored team from communist USSR. Commemorate this historic upset with a drink honoring the sweetness of victory!

Fill an eight-ounce glass with cubes of hockey ice.

Have Russian and American vodkas face off!

In your mixing container simultaneously pour in three ounces of Russian Vodka like Stoli and three ounces of an American Vodka such as Skyy. Feel free to use sweet-flavored vodkas like vanilla or birthday cake.

Mix it with a hockey stick (a popsicle stick will do).

Pour the vodka mix into your glass of hockey ice. Now drop the puck! (An Oreo cookie.)

If you like, top off the hockey game with a miracle ending of whipped cream. I love whipped cream. It is like heaven's clouds in a can.

Drink until the end of regulation, and then eat that delicious alcohol-soaked puck!

Act Out, Spazz Out

Have you ever wanted to be a Hollywood actor? Now is your chance! In this game you will act out scenes and get drunk, just like real Hollywood stars!

How to Play

The Shitfaced Referee will take scraps of paper and write an international sporting event and a country on each paper. For example, the one hundred–meter dash in Germany, the breaststroke in Canada, and so forth.

Divide everyone into two teams.

One player from each team is allowed to see the paper, and that player has to act out the card's country and sporting event. Each team must solve it correctly.

For instance, for weightlifting in Russia you can do the famous traditional Russian folk dance with the leg kicks and stomping, and then act out trying to pick up superheavy weights.

NOTE: **If you somehow bust out that black furry hat, you get one million bonus points and win at the game of life!**

If your team answers correctly within fifteen seconds, you earn five points. If it takes thirty seconds, then you get three points. If it takes sixty seconds, you add one point to your score. If you fail to answer correctly by the end of one minute, your turn is over, you get zero points, and everyone on your team must take a shot.

The team with the most points after five rounds is the winner! The losing team must take an extra shot to their pride, and by that I mean an extra shot of liquor!

EMBARRASSING ADMISSION: I once took a shot to my pride when I contacted this girl and she responded, "Are you trying to have a booty call?" So I backtracked and said, "It's not a booty call! I'm, uh, just asking if you want to release hormones to satiate our sexual urges and ironically amplify the feeling of loneliness. At 3 A.M."

Slap (Happy) Shots

You need a lot of space for this hockey game. This works well in a fraternity house, dorm, or foreclosed home that you've cleared of all meth addicts.

How to Play

Crush a beer can down into the form of a hockey puck. Most people will do this by stomping it with their foot—but you're not most people. You're smarter than that. You know it will be more impressive if you smash the can flat on your head. Chicks dig a dude with a semi-permanent beer ring on his forehead.

NOTE: **Next time empty the can first.**

In this game you will use brooms, mops, or hockey sticks as, er, hockey sticks.

Very basic hockey rules are in effect. Therefore, checking is okay but no high-sticking, hooking, or any foul play. Foul play includes things like kidney punching, titty twisting, uppercuts to the groin, and anything else you normally see in the NHL.

Play is stopped every two minutes for a toss-up question from the referee. A player from each team comes to the middle to answer.

The referee asks a question (trivia questions are fine, as are questions about people in your group), and the first player to throw his or her hand into the air gets to answer.

If he answers correctly, he stays in the game while the other player must leave the game to sit in the penalty box for the next two minutes and drink a beer. If he answers incorrectly, he leaves the game to the penalty box for the next two minutes, drinking the suds of the gods.

This causes a power play, in which one team has one less player on the "ice."

If neither player answers, they are both sent to the penalty box, and every member of both teams must do a shot.

Whenever you score a goal, every member of the other team must do a shot.

Decide beforehand if you will play one, two, or three twenty-minute periods.

The winner is the team with the most goals scored at the end of the game unless you decided to play three periods, in which case the winner is the team who can still stand!

Hockey is intense, and so are its fans! I have a buddy who would not even *speak* to his girl while a hockey game was on. Finally she left him. He asked me if it was maybe his fault, if he had a problem. So I told him, "No way, dude. It's totally normal to ignore your girlfriend so you can yell encouraging words to muscular men in uniform."

Alcohol Archery

I can't believe that archery is considered an official sport! Doing something skillful while standing is not a sport. If that were the case, I'd win a Gold medal for keeping my balance while reading on the bus at rush hour!

How to Play

I don't trust you drunkies with real bows and arrows, so for this version of alcohol archery you'll be using mini-arrows, also known as darts.

Actually, I have a cute female friend who is in a darts league! She's really cool, but in my experience usually people who play darts too seriously are *not* the people I want to throw darts with—they are the people I want to throw darts *at!*

Make two teams: white and black.

After a team hits all the numbers that have their color they must hit the bull's-eye. The team to accomplish this first wins.

Each time a player on your team misses your color or hits a number that has already been scratched off the board, each player on the team must drink half his beer.

The end of the game is where it gets really drunky, because each time your team misses the bull's-eye, everyone on your team must chug his entire beer. Your team wins when one of your players hits the bull's-eye.

I stink at darts because I am a dork! But I was an even bigger dork in high school. Back then my friends puked from drinking too much tequila. Meanwhile I would yell out, "I'm sick! It's because my apple juice is way too apple-y!"

Volleybeer

In my heaven there is a huge buffet of BBQ chicken wings, and we all party while watching hot girls play Olympic beach volleyball. Oh wait, I think that was a rap video. Same thing.

How to Play

Form two teams, and play volleyball! Here is how it gets you Shit-faced:

When someone on your team loses a point everyone on your team must drink some beer.

When someone on your team fails to get the serve over the net everyone on your team must chug an entire beer.

When someone on the other team hits the ball to someone on your team but it goes completely untouched, everyone on your team must chug an entire beer.

The first team to fifteen points is the winner!

LIFE NOTE: **If you want to be a winner at the game of life, learn how to enjoy yourself! Be happy you're alive! If you're dead, be happy that you're resting! If you're un-dead, be happy that you're eating brains!**

Pool Relay

This pool relay doesn't involve swimming; your relay will be at the pool table.

NOTE TO GUYS: **When a girl is standing in front of your target, don't yell out to her: "I'm gonna slam my balls into your pocket!" This will generally get you slapped in the face—by her foot. And as you lay on the pub's floor squirming in pain and spilled beer, she'll declare, "Two ball, from the corner pocket!" Then she'll step and twist on your groin-danglers as though she's extinguishing a cigarette.**

How to Play

Line up four balls in front of each of the four corner pockets. They should each be six inches straight in front of the pockets. Start at the scratch line and use a pool cue to knock in the first ball from across the table. Now your teammate grabs the pool cue and hits the second ball in, and so on.

Keep a timer for how long it takes your team to sink all four balls. The team with the fastest time is the winner! Each member of the losing team must do a shot.

Feel free to dress like a swimmer, but this might cause trouble if you play at your local tavern, as the roughnecks at Abnor O'Malley's Pub don't like men who flaunt their long, toned, shaved legs—they *love* them! Prepare to do the butterfly dance with guys named Razor, Rusty, Rocky, Ratchet, and Carl!

The Backstroke

A swimmer's body is a powerful, finely tuned machine. Your body makes you look like a hamster in a small T-shirt. Of course, no offense is intended toward hamsters. My pet hamster is quite athletic. And my hamster smokes pot. While high he told me his secret to being chubby yet still having fast legs: he coughed, "It's all in the joints!"

How to Play

Get the floor very slippery with something like vegetable oil or soapy water, or make good use of all those packets of duck sauce you've been hoarding from Chinese takeout!

Now oil up your body.

NOTE: Please wear a swimsuit or something. Don't slither across the floor naked, because unlike a snake, you can't shed your filthy skin afterward!

Two or more players compete to slide across the floor while doing the back stroke. The first to the finish line is the winner! The loser gulps a shot. Spectators bet on who will win. Everyone who bet wrong has to do a shot.

Now who's next to put their B.A.C. into their backstroke?!

SAFE-SEX PUBIC SERVICE ANNOUNCEMENT: Competitive swimmers don't use a full condom. They cover their heads with a tight white cap and put miniature Speedos over their balls. This has been a safe-sex pubic service announcement.

Ping-Pong Beer Bong

This drinking game is just like regular table tennis, but it is enhanced with delicious drinking!

Ping-Pong really is the perfect sport for me—no running, no jumping. And the skill is all in the wrist! Ha ha! Oh, wait, I think I just insulted myself. *Dammit!*

How to Play

Form two teams. In Round 1 send Player 1 from your team to battle Player 1 from the opposing team.

NOTE TO SELF: I'm not sure if "battle" is the correct verb for competitive Ping-Pong. Two people against each other in Ping-Pong is, at best, a squabble. It's actually not even a squabble. I've got it now . . .

In Round 1 send Player 1 to engage your opponent in a serious tiff. No, a *furious* tiff!

The winner of each round is the super-courageous Ping-Pong warrior who is first to eleven points. There are no tiebreakers, and you don't even have to win by two. Take *that* table-tennis traditionalists! We're drunk, and we don't give a flying forehand!

After one of the players is crowned the winner in Round 1, Player 2 from each team is the next to face off.

In the course of your Ping-Pong game here is when the drinking occurs:

When you lose a point you and everyone on your team must chug half a beer.

When you completely miss the ball or don't hit it at all on the return, you and your teammates must chug an entire beer. So if your team loses the game, your entire team will wind up chugging at *least* five and a half beers.

Before the match the teams will agree upon the number of rounds. So a three-round match could have you chugging sixteen and a half beers!

The winner is the team who has consumed the most beer, er, the team who wins the most games.

IMPORTANT NOTE: Did you know there are hot female Ping-Pong players?! It turns out that the hot female tennis player gene extends down to table tennis. Check out photos of table tennis's Biba Goli in her prime! It's crazy because usually when you see a hot chick doing amazing things with a Ping-Pong ball, she's not at the Olympics but instead at Big Sweaty Al's Strip Club: Home of Interstate 80's hottest exotic dancers and all-you-can-eat spaghetti!

SH*TFACED COCKTAIL

Jessie Owens Beats the Nazis

Celebrate the proudest moment in American Olympic history and perhaps international sports history! As the world looked on during the terror of Nazi Germany, Hitler was screaming about his superior race of Aryan people and promoting the extermination of who he saw as inferior races.

But when it came to an actual race, instead of his super-Nazi athletes being victorious, a black man representing everything he was trying to undo—democracy, tolerance, and the equality of all people— whooped them.

Honor Jesse Owens and his humiliation of Hitler with this drink!

8 ounces heavy German beer (such as Schwarzbier, Doppelbock, or Dunkles)
4 ounces Red Bull
$1/2$ ounce American whiskey (like Jim Beam)
$1/2$ ounce chocolate syrup

Fill a sixteen-ounce glass with the German beer and Red Bull to represent how Jesse Owens flew like he had wings against his German competition!

And because Jesse Owens was an American who shot Hitler's theories to hell, fill half of a shot glass with American whiskey. And because Jesse Owens was a proud chocolate man, fill the other half of the shot glass with chocolate syrup.

Wipe a bit of chocolate syrup under your nose to give yourself a Hitler mustache. Then drop the shot into the German beer! Now chug that drink until it washes that stupid mustache off Hitler's face!

To hell with Hitler! Besides, in the battle of Ruthless Dictatorial Facial Hair, Stalin had him beat! I imagine Stalin saying, "I vill crush zee Krauts. Zee Rooshan mustache iz zuperior to dat itty bitty thing on Heetler. My babooshka has more of a mustache!"

Wrestle for Beers

Wrestle for beers to prove you're not in the lightweight division!

How to Play

Cover your entire body in bubble wrap except for your groin and head. This means bubble wrap should completely protect your legs, arms, torso, and backside.

Opponents square off to wrestle. The object is to pop all of your opponent's bubbles!

This is Greco-Roman wrestling, not sumo wrestling—so no diapers!

NOTE: In America sumo wrestlers don't get paid nearly as much as their giant counterparts—offensive linemen in the NFL. American sumos are doing it for the love of giving wedgies! It would be cool if sumo wrestlers had "finishing moves," like slapping your exhausted opponent in the face with a large slice of ham.

To pop those bubbles, pin down your rival! Slap those bubbles until they pop! Pop 'em with wrestling moves! Remember, there is no kicking or punching in wrestling—just good clean groping, er, grappling!

There are three two-minute rounds. After each round, chug a beer.

ANOTHER NOTE ABOUT SUMO WRESTLING BECAUSE MY DRUNK MIND IS MEANDERING: I don't think sumo wrestlers should ever inject steroids—they should inject themselves with baked

beans! Imagine the thunderous internal explosions! I want to see a sumo wrestler hold his opponent's face to his barely covered blubbery butt and fire off his huge stink cannon. It would be awesome to see the skin on the other guy's face blow back as though he was a dog with his head hanging out the car window on the highway.

NOTE TO SELF: You're supposed to puke from drinking, not from the disgusting images you come up with!

At the end of the complete six-minute match the judge determines who popped the most bubbles and is, therefore, the winner. The loser must chug an extra beer to help wash down his shame.

Ya know, it's amazing that no one from the International Sumo Wrestling Commission has hired me—or forced me to wear an adult diaper while slapping me in the face with a large slice of pig meat!

DRINKING FACT: Seventy percent of people with blood alcohol content over 0.1 cannot do simple math. The other 50 percent are just idiots.

Shot Put Eggs Until You Vomelet!

In some places around the world the people don't have enough food to eat. Don't think about that while playing this game, which has you hurling perfectly good food while sucking down liquor.

How to Play

While holding a shot of liquor in one hand, use your other hand to shot put an egg to your teammate. You must throw the egg like a shot putter.

Your teammate must catch the egg with one hand while holding his shot of liquor in his other hand, and he must not spill the shot or drop the egg. If either occurs, your team loses the round and you both must drink your shots.

Play as many rounds as you can stand!

NOTE: **Playing this drinking game with Easter eggs is highly inappropriate.**

THINGS I SAY WHEN HUNGOVER: **"Ugh, alcohol is the devil's poison. Thank God for the antidote: bacon and eggs. What do you mean bacon and eggs clog your arteries? The devil hath fooled me again!"**

Dice Hockey

In many role-playing games you can take on fictional characters of great strength, bravery, and magical powers such as the Mighty Orc or a half-elf princess. In this drinking role-playing game you take on the personas of mystical hockey players such as the Toothless Gnome and the Wincing Warlock.

How to Play

You will need two dice and a shot that you can manage to drink up to ten times.

Everyone chooses a hockey character.

Each hockey character has differing strengths in three important aspects.

V = Vitality

S = Speed

P = Power

Choose one of these hockey characters:

Enforcer: V: 9; S: 1; P: 10

Pretty-Boy Scorer: V: 8; S: 10; P: 2

Playmaker: V: 8; S: 9; P: 3

Pest: V: 9; S: 6; P: 5

Grinder: V: 10; S: 4; P: 6

You're out of the game when your vitality is zero. The winner is the last remaining hockey character.

Two players face off and roll the dice. Each time you lose you lose one vitality point and must drink a shot.

Player 1 rolls the two dice and then decides if he will apply the sum of his dice to his speed or power points. For example, Player 1 is a Grinder and rolls a seven. He then applies those seven points to his six power points: $7 + 6 = 13$.

Then Player 2 rolls the dice and must apply the sum to the same category that Player 1 chose. So if Player 2 is a Pest and rolls a nine, she applies those nine points to her five power points: $9 + 5 = 14$. Fourteen is greater than thirteen, so the Pest wins the round! The loser of this round subtracts one point from his Vitality total and does a shot. In our example, the Grinder now subtracts one from his ten vitality points: $10 - 1 = 9$. In the case of a tie the winner will be the player who rolled their dice second.

Now Player 2 gets to go first to challenge someone else. (You can't challenge the player who just challenged you unless no one else is left.)

Another example makes the game very easy to follow:

The Enforcer rolls the dice first. He rolls a seven. He decides to use his power to defeat his opponent. Now his ten power points become seventeen power points.

His opponent is a Pretty-Boy Scorer who also rolls a seven. He must use his power because that was the category chosen. He has two power points: $7 + 2 = 9$. That's not enough because the Enforcer has seventeen. Pretty-Boy Scorer loses! His vitality drops one point: $8 - 1 = 7$. He must take a shot.

Now it's Pretty-Boy Scorer's turn to go first, and he decides whom to challenge. The strategy is in whom you choose to challenge and which category you choose. But are you sober enough to figure it out?! By the end of the game you won't be sober enough to remember the name on the back of your own jersey!

Got that, Kjerti Romanski?

GOLD-MEDAL
DRINKING
GAMES

Tongues on Ice

In this international hockey-themed game, if you screw up the tongue twister, you will be subjected to "icing."

How to Play

Do a shot of vodka, then attempt a terrifying tongue twister at a torrid tempo!

If you get tangled up in the tongue twister, "icing" means you must close your eyes and someone will shock you with an ice cube to the neck, down your clothes, or so forth.

There are ten terrific tongue-twisting rounds.

Each round features a different tongue twister that all players must attempt to say quickly:

Round 1: Poland's puck on the power play pushed past Petersen's pad.

Round 2: Official overtime occurs only after perfunctory periods pass and scores are equal thus only a sequel will seal a victorious victory for the victors occurring alongside a vexing punishment for second place.

Round 3: Slovakian Skater Andrej Sekera slapped the puck to teammate Andrej Nedorost who slid past Swedes swishing, swooshing, swooshing, swishing, sticking, swishing, swooshing until sliding and gliding and guiding the puck past the pads of the goalie for a Slovakian score to soar the score past the Swedes.

Round 4: The Swiss superbly resist a far-flung wrist flick.

Round 5: The Swiss subs swagger, superbly sliding like soap, swatting sundry Swedish scoring squabbles.

Round 6: Petersen picked Piker's puck and passed the pill with pistol-piercing perfection, plopping Puggerman on his portly posterior.

Round 7: Hockey is faster than a donkey doing the hokey pokey dance holding a handsome pig.

Round 8: He shoots, he scores! He scores, he shoots! His girlfriend is pregnant because they didn't use safety equipment.

Round 9: Orator Orville Oppenheimer oscillates on the ice. Orville Oppenheimer handily operates huge Zamboni machines to clear the ice on official time-outs. Oh, that Orville Oppenheimer opines overbearing oratories of observations while munching macaroni mixed with overly zesty cheddar cheese.

Round 10: France fought off Finland, Russia romped Romania, America ass whooped Australia, Germany jumped past Japan, China cooked Chile, and Denmark defeated the Dominican Republic. As for Hungary and Honduras, who has hockey's upper hand?

By the end of this game everyone will have ingested ten shots of vodka, and some players will have suffered a frostbitten zesty zing zapping their zipped-up zoo parts.

Kissing the Medal

Kissing the medal on the winner's stage is a fine tradition. With that in mind, in this drinking game you will kiss!

How to Play

Get in a circle of guys and girls who don't mind having to kiss someone else in the group.

In other words, this might exclude faithful couples who aren't trying to get all kinky as well as people who believe that kissing is something sacred to be saved for their English teacher's ass.

Draw a card from a playing deck. If you draw a number card, you drink hard alcohol such as tequila or vodka. But if it's a face card, you will have to kiss the next opposite-sex person (or just next person, depending on how your friends roll) who randomly draws a face card.

When an opposite-sex player draws a face card she draws one more card. If her new card is a Jack, Queen, King, or Ace, the kiss has to be with tongue; otherwise it's a kiss on the lips.

Guys, if it's going to be a tongue kiss, get passionate and make all the girls in the room get hot with your manly control of the situation! Put your face on her neck and kiss your lips against her feminine skin. Inhale her scent. Bite her. Lick behind her ear. Stroke her hair. Gently breathe in her ear. Moan, "You smell sooooo good." Grunt with desire. Make manly noises like "[*Belch!*] Sorry babe, too much beer!"

To help illustrate:

Sally picks a nine. She drinks.

Tom picks a queen. He waits to see whom he will be smooching.

Carlos picks a king. He doesn't drink and doesn't have to kiss.

Lacy picks a two. She drinks.

Pete picks a four. He drinks.

Rebecca picks a king. She will be kissing Tom. She picks another card. It's an Ace, so she has to kiss Tom with tongue.

Because being forced to kiss in front of all your friends isn't embarrassing enough, pile it on! When two people have to kiss, everyone should clink silverware against their drinking glasses like it's a wedding kiss! Understandably, some players will be too uptight to appreciate this gesture. In that case, practice mature decorum by averting your eyes while making exaggerated kissy sounds!

WARNING: Drunk kissing may lead to drunk dancing! And drunk dancing is like drunk sex: yes, alcohol makes it more likely to happen but also more likely you'll flop around wildly and spill something.

Sports Motion Sickness

Choose a sporting event and a motion or gesture to represent it!

How to Play

Choose an athletic event such as diving and make a diving motion, or choose javelin and represent it with a throw, or select Judo and grapple with the shortest person in your group by choking him.

NOTE: Just kidding. Don't grapple. It is a cool word though, now that I know what it means. For about ten years I thought it was a Snapple flavor.

When someone calls out your sporting event, you must—without hesitation—do your move or else you must drink vodka. After you do your move you will call out someone else's event and do their gesture without hesitation.

Keep the pace of the game moving fast to trip people up and make them drink! And remember: it's not Snapple but alcohol that's made from the best stuff on earth! Drink up! It's good for you!

NOTE: It's good for you unless you're the unlucky short person in your group getting assaulted by your drunken friends attempting their clumsy Judo moves on you!

Man, I realize that I drink so much that I've gone from being ashamed of it to taking pride in it—much like the nation of Ireland.

I Figure You're Skating on Thin Ice!

Why is figure skating so popular? Is it the graceful dancing? Is it the skill and technique? Nah, it's the tight butts! I prefer a girl with some curves. I once dated a girl who was too skinny! One time she farted and broke her hip.

How to Play

Put your right hand in. Put your right hand out. Put your right hand in and shake it all about. Oh wait, wrong word processor window. I also write children's books.

Begin by drinking a shot.

Roll a die.

If you roll a one or a two, you must jump and twist 360 degrees in the air.

Rolling a three or a four means you must throw your arms up in the victory pose while standing on one leg.

Roll a five or a six, and you will twirl with your feet on the ground with lots of little steps.

Immediately after your figure skating move slurp a shot without spilling.

If you fall or spill, then you are out. The last figure skater standing wins the medal!

I have a friend who insists that all male figure skaters are gay because they twirl around in tight pants. So I brought up football players. I reminded him: "They twirl around in tight little pants too. Except they'll stop for a group hug."

He yelled back at me: "They're not *twirling*! It's called a spin move! And they're not getting a hug—they're being tackled by men!"

So I said to him: "Everything you know about football comes from video games. And I know you play way too many video games because your girlfriend told me that whenever you get an erection, you make the Super Mario sound." Then he threw a fireball at me, pulled my spine out of my skin, and bellowed, "Fatality!"

Marathon Drinking

NOTE TO PEOPLE WHO WANT TO RUN A MARATHON: I understand your need to prove to yourself that you can run 26.2 miles in one go. That said, doing so is entirely impractical and stupid. So for everyone's benefit, I know a wonderful restaurant that is 13.1 miles away from my house but does not deliver. Marathon your ass over there and get me some lunch!

How to Play

Instead of twenty-six miles, this marathon drinking game will last for twenty-six minutes. The winner is the drinking athlete who can make it to the end of the game without puking!

The marathon is named after the famous Greek myth in which Marathenius runs from Athens to Helena during the War of Souvlaki to deliver a lamb gyro. Upon delivering it to the floor of the Senate, he fell dead in the arms of Socrates. He could not be revived in the customary manner of eating chocolate baklava.

NOTE: I'm betting that 0 percent of you reading this book are history majors. But if you are, stick those facts in your pipe and smoke them while wearing your comfy-looking sweater in your leather chair surrounded by books!

All contestants must drink one shot of beer in the first minute.

Then everyone must drink two shots of beer during the second minute.

Everyone drinks three shots of beer during the third minute.

This continues until you take ten shots of beer during the tenth minute.

Then you coast along by drinking five shots of beer every minute thereafter until the end of the twenty-sixth minute.

If you belch, then you must drink an extra shot.

If you fail to drink all your shots of beer in the corresponding minute, you are disqualified. You are also disqualified if you vomit.

HINT: Try to get others to vomit by trash talking after drinking your shots! For example: "I feel great! You probably feel the opposite, like being on a ship rocking back and forth on the ocean water with the sun beating down on you and someone is force feeding you spoiled Greek yogurt. The smell of curdled dairy gets trapped in your nose, and the waves push you back and forth, side to side, and a seagull craps on your head. Whatever you do, don't puke! Sure, it will relieve the pain and make you feel better right away. But don't puke! Especially because there will be chunks of undigested lamb balls! That's right. Your gyro was made of big, furry lamb testicles."

The winner will make it through minute twenty-six and shout, "Holy Moussaka!"

NOTE: The unofficial winner is the loser who got revenge on the trash talker by hitting him in the face with his projectile vomit!

DRINKING FACT: Alcohol dehydrates you, which causes stress. Luckily for you, beer is mostly water. So be sure to drink plenty of beer to compensate for those other beers!

Dice Volleyball–Bump, Set, Spike the Punch!

Volleyball has become one of the most-watched Olympic sports, mainly because the wedgies on the women are fantastic. (No offense to the sexy wedgies on the sumo wrestlers.)

How to Play

In this game you will be drinking spiked punch or Jell-O spiked with liquor. I'm not ashamed to admit that I'm a grown man who loves Jell-O shots!

So when do you guzzle a shot of spiked punch? Every time the other team wins a point!

Dice Volleyball is best played one-on-one or two-on-two when players take turns rolling the dice.

Team 1 starts with a serve by rolling one of the dice.

Team 2 shouts, "Bump!" Then they roll two dice. If Team 2's dice add up to less than Team 1's roll, they immediately lose the point, and Team 2 must take a spiked shot of punch!

If Team 2's dice are equal to or greater than Team 1's roll, they shout, "Set!" and roll the dice again. If the roll adds up to less than six, the set has failed, and Team 2 loses the point and must take a spiked shot of punch!

But if Team 2's dice add up to six or more, it was a successful set, so now they shout, "Spike!" and roll the dice. They add up the dice, and now Team 1 attempts to block.

Team 1 will roll two dice in their block attempt. If Team 1's dice add up to less than Team 2's, Team 1 loses the point and the ball so they must drink, and Team 2 will serve next.

But if Team 1's dice add up to more than Team 2's, Team 1 wins the point and keeps the ball to serve again.

If Team 1's dice add up to the same amount as Team 2's, the ball is still in play, and Team 2 will shout, "Bump!" and do it all again.

For example, let's call the two teams the Brazilian Full Moons and the American Legcellence.

Team Full Moons serves by rolling one die. It's a four. Team Legsellence shouts, "Bump!" and they roll two dice that add up to seven. It's a successful bump! So they shout, "Set!" and roll again, and this time the dice add up to five. That's less than six, so Legsellence loses the point and must drink the spiked punch.

The game is played to fifteen points, and just like in the Olympics, you must win by at least two points more than the other team.

That sounded all official-like! After all, getting Shitfaced is serious business! Now if you'll excuse me, I have a high-level meeting with Dr. Pepper and his associates, Mr. Jack Daniels, Mr. Jim Beam, and Señor Jose Cuervo. We're planning to close a big deal. But honestly, it'll probably wind up in the toilet. *Puuuuuuke!*

SH*TFACED COCKTAIL

A Shameful Johnson

Ben Johnson was once the world's fastest human.

But he was found guilty of doping, stripped of all his records and Gold medals, and disgraced, embarrassing his nation of Canada. So for this Shitfaced Cocktail:

Fill a pint glass with a Canadian beer such as Molson. Mix in Canadian maple syrup from the maple leaf nation. Chug it fast with the speed of Ben Johnson! Let everyone know you drank highly sweetened beer like a pansy-ass! Now you've experienced the shame of Ben Johnson!

Shots on Goal!

Everybody loves ice hockey! And by everybody, I mean people who live in cold countries that suck at basketball. Ha ha!

How to Play

In this drinking game you will be getting "pucked up" (see what I did there?) by playing three-on-three hockey with one referee.

Each of the two teams will have three players: a goalie, a forward, and a defenseman.

To begin this game the two forwards face off! Each forward drinks a shot. Whomever downs their drink first, according to the referee, advances, and his team now has possession of the virtual puck. That team can boastfully shout, "Puck off!" to their opponent.

NOTE: I promise there are only forty-seven more puck puns. Give me a pucking break, okay?

Now the winning forward steps up to drink against the opposing team's defenseman. Again, whoever drinks the shot the fastest advances. So if the forward finishes first again, he again advances to face off against the opposing team's goalie. But if the defenseman finishes first, the puck is passed to his forward, who will now face off against the opposing team's defenseman.

Whenever a goalie is up, the opposing team must shout, "Shot on goal!" And if the shooting team scores, exclaim, "Puck yeah!"

Ah, pucking hell, I did it again.

When a goalie loses a face-off the other team scores a goal. The game goes on for fifteen minutes. If, at the end of the fifteen-minute regulation period, there is a tie, then there are penalty shots, mother-pucker! Then each team's goalie will face off against each of the three players on the other team. This continues until there is a winning team.

NOTE: If players are amateur drinkers, it's smart to allow for team substitutions so nobody suffers a brain injury. In other words, after a player has consumed many drinks in a short time, substitute in someone from the bench to take his place.

NOTE ABOUT THAT LAST NOTE: If someone suffers brain damage, he is now qualified to be a professional hockey player.

Skeet Shot

In Olympic skeet shooting a clay disc is fired into the air and the player uses his skeet gun to shoot it.

These guys train their whole lives to shoot falling brown discs in midair! Why are these sharp shooters not having their skills employed year round?!

Every major city should hire skeet shooters to destroy falling discs of bird doody before they hit our cars or shoulders or become sprinkles on our ice cream! Ew! Ha ha!

How to Play

In this version of the skeet shot, two players will face off. Player 1 is the skeet shooter, so he holds a toy water gun full of liquor. Player 2 tries to get Player 1 to "miss" the discs. To begin, Player 2 allows Player 1 to see a coin that is placed under one of three opaque "skeet shot" glasses.

Player 2 then quickly moves the glasses around for about ten seconds, trying to confuse the already-tipsy Player 1. While the disc (coin) is being rotated around, onlookers must shout, "Skeet skeet skeet!"

If, on the first try, Player 1 guesses which glass is hiding the disc, Player 2 loses and must fill the three glasses with liquor and swallow the three shots as everyone chants, "Swallow that skeet!" Plus, Player 1 must shoot liquor from his skeet pistol into Player 2's mouth.

But if Player 1 fails to find the disc on the first try, then he must take the three shots.

The players then switch roles.

Now the next two party people face off or go for a rematch if you can manage to skeet again!

Snowboarding Tricks for Treats

In the Olympic snowboarding half-pipe event, tricks are evaluated and rewarded with points. These tricks have silly names such as Chicken Salad, Beef Curtains, Bloody Dracula, Nosegrab, and Swiss Cheese Air.

Because you're drunk, there's no way I'll encourage you to do something so physically challenging while in your current state of being mentally challenged. Instead, our version will include coin tricks with silly names while you are dressed as a snowboarder.

These tricks are tricky because you'll be wearing goggles and mittens.

NOTE TO SELF: Did you just say, "These tricks are tricky?" Ugh! You're stupider than, um, something that's really stupid! . . . Dammit!

How to Play

Each snowboarding trick varies in difficulty, so each has a different number of points that you can earn. The team with the most points at the end wins, which was what I told the judge when he added more points to my driver's license for speeding.

The strategy is to choose between easier, lower-scoring tricks or harder, higher-scoring tricks.

Set up a table with a shot glass, coffee mug, beer mug, and beer pitcher.

Before your attempt you must announce the name of the trick you are attempting.

TRICK NAME: The Spins

While wearing your mittens, you spin a coin. It must spin for at least five seconds without falling off the table. After the five seconds you must pick it up with your mitten hands without dropping it.

Success means you get one hundred points for the round.

Failure means everyone on your team takes a shot.

TRICK NAME: Get It In

With your mitten hands, toss the coin into a container on the table while standing six feet away.

Sinking it into the beer pitcher gets you ten points.

Landing it in the beer mug gets you fifty points.

Tossing it in the coffee mug gets you one hundred points.

Getting it in the shot glass is worth five hundred points.

If you want to earn double the points, allow the other team(s) to shoot you in your goggles with water guns while you toss the coin. If it's the last round and you're losing by one thousand points, this may be your only chance!

Failure to get the coin in any container results in every member of your team consuming a shot.

TRICK NAME: Shiny Tip Grabber

While wearing your mittens, bend your arm toward you and place the shiny metal coin on the tip of your elbow. Quickly throw your hand down to catch the coin before it falls to the floor.

Success gets you one hundred points.

Failure means you and your teammates must take a shot.

An opposing team flips the coin. While in the air, you guess heads or tails.

If you guess correctly, you earn fifty points and can go again. If you guess incorrectly, everyone on your team must drink a shot.

The opposing team flips the coin for a second time, and if your guess is correct again, you win another one hundred points on top of your first fifty. If your guess is incorrect, everyone on your team takes a shot.

You can quit now or have the opposing team flip for a third and final time. If you guess correctly on the third flip, you earn an additional 1,000 points. But if you're wrong on the third flip, you lose the 150 points you've earned previously in this round, and everyone on your team must take a shot.

The team with the most points after five rounds is the winner!

Believe me, this game will get you pretty drunk, and your friends will find out if you're a happy, angry, or silly drunk. My grandpa is the type to get all sentimental when he's drunk. After drinking, he once said to me: "What happened to me? I used to ride a motorcycle, wear a leather jacket, and get all the babes! Oh wait, that wasn't me—that was the Fonz."

The Drinking Triathlon

It's the drinking triathlon of beer, wine, and liquor!

And what goes with drinkin'? Tacos!

How to Play

The winner is the last athlete standing. If you give up or puke, you are out.

Round 1

Each contestant eats a taco. You have one minute to eat the taco or you're out. You then must chug a beer in thirty seconds or you are out.

Round 2

Each contestant eats a taco in under one minute, then guzzles a glass of wine. You have thirty seconds to guzzle the wine or you are out.

Round 3

Each contestant eats a taco in under one minute then must down a shot of liquor. You have fifteen seconds to do your shot.

The rounds repeat with the beer, wine, and liquor until there is one person left who has not given up or vomited.

Hey, you know what they say: beer before liquor with beans in fried tortilla . . . lots of diarrhea . . . liquor with Mexican food before beer . . . you'll be puking out your rear.

Either way this game is a blast! Heh heh—blast.

SH*TFACED COCKTAIL

The Insane Usain

Celebrate Usain Bolt,
the fastest human ever, with this shot.

Fill a pint glass with beer from Usain Bolt's home nation of Jamaica, such as Red Stripe.

Fill a shot glass with Jamaican rum such as Myers's.

If you run against Usain Bolt, he's going to leave you in his dust! So sprinkle on a dusting of cinnamon.

Add two dashes of grain alcohol to the shot glass.

Usain Bolt is going to light you up! He runs like he's on fire! So light the drink on fire!

Yell out: "On your mark, get set, go!" Now drop the shot into the glass of beer (the beer will extinguish the flame!), take a deep breath, and chug!

Did you take down Usain Bolt,
or did he smoke you from the inside?

Basketball Fowl Shots

DID YOU KNOW: In a parallel universe basketball players with conservative haircuts cheer for tatted-up accountants when they complete financial reports.

How to Play

In this Shitfaced Games basketball version you will turn foul shots into fowl shots.

If you don't have a real hoop, you can do this with a Nerf basketball or paper balls and a garbage can.

This game requires fowl in the form of chicken fingers as well as shots of alcohol.

Players line up to do foul/fowl shots.

You may attempt your foul/fowl shot in a regular shooting position, underhanded, or with your back to the basket.

BASKETBALL PLAYER OBSERVATION: So many of today's basketball players are covered in tattoos! I wouldn't be surprised if this conversation has happened:

COACH: Williams, turn around, I need to check something. Thanks again for letting me tattoo the playbook on your back.

WILLIAMS: No problem, Coach. It's where you tattooed the roster that was weird!

Regular shooting position: If you make it, you get one point, and everyone else must drink a shot and eat chicken. If you miss it, everyone else gets one point, and you must drink a shot and eat chicken.

Underhanded shooting position: If you make it, you get two points, and everyone must drink two shots and eat two pieces of chicken. If you miss it, everyone else gets two points, and you must drink two shots and eat two pieces of chicken.

Back to the basket position: If you make it, you get ten points and everyone else must drink three shots and eat three pieces of chicken. If you miss it, everyone else gets ten points and you must drink three shots and eat three pieces of chicken.

After five rounds (five foul shots each), the winner is the player with the most points, provided he did not throw up. Technical fowl—ha ha!

Whatever you do, don't throw up on your basketball sneakers! That is some expensive footwear! Basketball sneaker fashion is big business, but it seems that they're running out of innovative ideas for the huge shoes of pro basketball players. I think they should make a size-29 shoe that is fully equipped with ABS brakes, power steering, and an aquarium in the heel.

IMPORTANT BASKETBALL FASHION NOTE: I think any male basketball player who wears those stupid knee-high socks should be forced to wear the rest of the Catholic schoolgirl uniform!

Dope Supplier

International sports have very strict testing policies to ensure against players using performance enhancing drugs, known colloquially as doping. But even still, some athletes will try to get an illegal advantage. In this game the Doping Cop must catch the Dope Dealer.

DOPING FACT: Steroids have been around since nearly the beginning of Olympic competition. While preparing for the triathlon in the 210 B.C. Olympics, Juicingus Maximus experimented with different strength formulas.

Back then not only was it important to be strong but also to look good because the Olympic athletes competed while totally nude.

Maximus tried all of the standard Ancient Greek methods of increasing strength, such as making love to his sheep. But this time he tried something different and ate a pair of bull testicles. It made his muscles grow while at the same time made his own testicles shrink. Bonus! Because now he was stronger *and* had less wind resistance while running naked!

How to Play

To begin, count out the same number of playing cards as you have participants—the more drinkers, the more challenging the game! So if you have twelve drinkers, shuffle twelve cards and have each person pick his random card and keep it a secret. There must be exactly one king and one ace in the cards.

The person who picks the king is the Cop, and the person who selects the ace is the Dope Dealer. Everyone else is an athlete.

Everyone holds a beer.

The object is for the Cop to catch the Dope Dealer within five minutes. The Dope Dealer's goal is to complete as many deals as possible in those five minutes.

To complete a deal the Dope Dealer will make eye contact with an athlete and wink. After the wink the athlete takes a generous gulp of beer. The Dope Dealer may drink whenever she wants to throw off the Cop. Other participants may drink at any time they please.

As soon as the Cop thinks he knows the Dope Dealer's identity, he accuses her. If the Cop is correct, the Dope Dealer must drink one shot for every minute remaining in the game. For instance, if the Cop correctly names the Dope Dealer when there are three minutes left in the game, the Dope Dealer loses and must drink three shots. If the Cop is wrong, the Cop takes a shot and the game continues.

If the game goes the full five minutes, the Cop has to make a guess. If correct, the Dope Dealer loses and takes a shot. If the Cop is still wrong, he must take shots. How many shots? Half the number of the dope deals that were made! So if the Dope Dealer winked at ten athletes during the game and never got caught, the Cop who couldn't catch him must drink five shots!

When athletes are busted for performance-enhancing drugs, officials often put an asterisk next to their names in the record books. Instead of the asterisk, I think they should put tiny testicles to represent their shrinkage from taking steroids!

Wives of disgraced athletes have commented to the media: "My husband has tiny, tiny balls from using steroids. That's okay—he's big in his pants where it counts . . . in his wallet!"

And sometimes the athletes will express remorse and try to become good role models for children by going into classrooms to say, "Remember kids, don't do drugs. Don't do drugs, kids. Kids, don't do drugs, or I will break into a steroid raaaaaage!"

SH*TFACED COCKTAIL

Swimming in Medals

No one has won more Olympic medals than
Michael Phelps. So let's toast to his
success by drinking the gold, silver, and bronze!

Fill an eight-ounce glass with bronze-colored beer.

Add a shot of Silver Patron tequila.

Add a shot of Goldschläger or gold tequila.

Stir it up until that alcohol is splashing around the glass! This drink will get you so Shitfaced you'll be swimming laps on someone's lap!

Boxing Punch

To be honest, I'm not a huge fan of boxing. I haven't seen a boxing match since that crazy guy with the face tattoo ate his opponent's ear in the ring. But this drinking game is about what we all love about boxing—the punch!

How to Play

It's a one-on-one boxing match, so start with some trash talking! And get a bowl of spiked punch ready!

Ya know, if I were a boxer, I'd get my ass beat. But I would outsmart my opponent with reverse psychology trash talking. Instead of calling my opponent a sissy-boy with an ugly wife, I'd be all compliments to confuse him.

Me: My opponent, Mr. Carlos de la Coma, is a great man. He's the best boxer today. His family is genetically superior. And the man knows how to dress.

De La Coma: Uh, hmm. Well, uh, my opponent is going down in two rounds! I want blood!

Me: Did I mention that Mr. de la Coma is a charitable and generous person who donates his time and money to help orphaned children?

De La Coma: Uh, thanks, man. I, uh, hm, no one has ever been this

nice to me. Forget the fight. I'm going to buy you ice cream!

See, I'd be a classy boxer. So much so that I'd box wearing tuxedo cufflinks.

Boxing is a game of power, precision, and stamina. And you also need to be able to take a punch! In this case, the punch will be the strong alcoholic kind.

But above all you must have the will to win. Do you have it in you? And when it's in you, will you puke it out?

There are three rounds. The first fighter who wins two rounds is the champion.

Shuffle a deck of cards. Boxer 1 picks the top card and shows it to "throw his punch." Then Boxer 2 picks the next card and shows it to decide the outcome.

If Boxer 1's card is greater than Boxer 2's card, then the punch has landed and Boxer 1 scores a point. Because a point has been scored, the loser of the point must drink a shot of the strong punch.

If Boxer 2's card is greater, he scores the point, so Boxer 1 must take a shot of punch.

If the cards are the same value, each boxer must take a shot of the punch and then draw new cards until someone scores.

The round is complete when one boxer has scored three points. Then the cards are reshuffled for the next round.

To add a bit of strategy, each boxer is allowed to throw one "knock-out punch" in the match. Before choosing a card the boxer shouts, "knock-out punch!" If his card is greater than his opponent's, the round ends immediately in his favor, and the opposing boxer must take three shots of punch.

But if his knock-out punch card is lower or the same value as his opponent's, he immediately loses the round and must take three extra shots of punch.

You are not required to use your knock-out punch during each match, but there are times when you certainly need to!

SOMETHING I JUST REALIZED: **If you asked me to name three recent boxers, I would tell you Mike Tyson, Evander Holyfield, and King Hippo from *Mike Tyson's Punch-out*.**

When you lose a round you must take another shot of punch. When you lose the entire match you must take a final shot of punch.

But you won't lose; you're gonna be the toast of the town! Because you can't spell champagne without the champ! Except we're drinking some wacky fruit concoction full of moonshine. But whatevz—you get the idea!

Being on the boxing champion's team is great. But it sucks to be the guy who has to lift the champion on his shoulders and have the back of his head pressed against the champ's swollen, sweaty groin-danglers. Ew!

Ski-Jump Crash and Burn

The Ski-Jump Crash and Burn awards points for distance and style. So form two teams ready to go the distance in style! And by style, I mean you're wearing a shirt that hides beer drool.

How to Play

Each team creates their own "crash-and-burn" drink. Try to make this drink as powerful and as gross tasting as possible—it should make the other team crash and burn as it goes down their throats!

Use lots of different alcohols, odd mixers, hot sauce—anything edible!

Now Team 1 will perform their Ski Jump.

Each member of your team downs an easy-to-drink shot such as coconut rum or flavored vodka. Do this in succession: Player 1 downs the shot, then Player 2 immediately does his or her shot, and so on. Once all team members have taken their shots, Player 1 jumps forward as far as possible. Then Player 2 leaps forward, and so on. Stay in your new locations.

Style points: if anyone falls down during his jump attempt, meaning he didn't land cleanly because he fell on his butt or tipped over, the team loses ten points and that skier has crashed and burned, so he must slowly drink a gulp of the other team's revolting crash-and-burn drink.

The players on Team 1 who jumped the least and most distance stay in their positions. Everyone else is excused.

Now Team 2 drinks their easy shot one after the other. Now they each jump forward, one after the other. Every player who falls subtracts ten style points from the team's score and must savor a gulp of the nasty crash-and-burn drink the opposing team created.

The team with the skier who jumped the furthest gets fifty points. The team with the skier who jumped the least distance loses twenty points.

The winner of the round is the team with the most points. Every member of the team who lost that round must gulp from the opposing team's crash-and-burn drink.

Play three rounds. At the end of three rounds every member of the losing team must gulp from that team's *own* crash-and-burn drink to get a taste of their own medicine!

SH*TFACED COCKTAIL

Spain is Faking It

In the 2000 Summer Paralympics, Spain was found guilty of cheating. How? The Paralympics is for athletes with disabilities. In the event for intellectually disabled basketball, Spain had their players fake having IQs under 70. Spain did this in numerous other events, so they had to return all the medals they had won fraudulently.

Let us never forget this outrageous act of shameful behavior of faking it.

And that's why we will take the famous Spanish drink sangria and fake it!

Real sangria requires red wine, sliced fruit, like apples and oranges, brandy, and soda. But to make fake Spanish sangria, all you need to do is fill a bucket with Kool-Aid and vodka and then throw in a handful of fruit. Done!

Don't Be a Loser— Guess the Winner!

The key to life is knowledge. And when you lack knowledge, the key to life is to be a good guesser! In this game you will test your skills at "eeny meeny miny moe alcohol please!"

How to Play

Refer to the list of men's Olympic Gold-medal hockey team winners by year at the end of this game. The referee will then ask each drinking-game team to name the winning nation of a particular year at random, then he will cross out that year and proceed.

Two teams battle in this game of trivia, drinking, and drinking.

NOTE: There will also be some drinking.

NOTE ABOUT SAFE DRINKING AND HOCKEY: Do not drink and drive . . . a Zamboni machine. That would be too much fun.

NOTE TO PEOPLE ASKING THEMSELVES, WHAT THE HECK IS A ZAMBONI MACHINE?: It's a large, four-wheel vehicle that makes pasta.

NOTE TO SELF: That would be so cool! I'd love to see hockey players slipping on fettuccini and slapping ravioli into the crowd!

The team with the most correct answers after all the Olympic years are exhausted is the winner.

If your team loses the round, don't hang your head, *lift* your head and take a shot!

HINT: As of the printing of this book, only the following nations have won a Gold medal in men's hockey: Canada, Czech Republic, Europe Unified Team, Great Britain, Soviet Union, Sweden, and the United States.

ANOTHER HINT: Always floss after eating broccoli.

Olympic Gold-Medal Hockey Team Winners

1920 Canada	1972 Soviet Union
1924 Canada	1976 Soviet Union
1928 Canada	1980 USA
1932 Canada	1984 Soviet Union
1936 Great Britain	1988 Soviet Union
1948 Canada	1992 Europe Unified Team
1952 Canada	1994 Sweden
1956 Soviet Union	1998 Czech Republic
1960 USA	2002 Canada
1964 Soviet Union	2006 Sweden
1968 Soviet Union	2010 Canada

Shot Put . . . Down Your Throat

Marla Runyan is a three-time 5,000-meter US national champion and the first-ever legally blind athlete to compete in the Olympics.

The athlete qualified for the Olympics despite many near-tragedies. She almost got decapitated while racing the hurdles, she nearly ran into a javelin, and she came dangerously close to extinguishing the Olympic torch when she lost her way while searching for the restroom.

In her honor, players will compete in this drinking event while blindfolded. The object of this game is for the blindfolded person to guess the type of alcohol he's drinking.

How to Play

Divide everyone into teams of two. One person on each team wears the blindfold, and the other person will help the blind person guess the alcohol.

Someone on another team pours the shot so everyone except the blindfolded person can see what it is. The blindfolded person will have three chances to name the alcohol correctly.

If the blindfolded person doesn't guess it correctly after drinking the shot, he must drink it again. At this time the teammate can give one hint, such as: "The shot you just drank is what you had that time you accidentally sent a drunk text to your grandma that was meant for your ex-girlfriend."

If the player still fails to name the alcohol, he must take another shot of this same alcohol and his partner may give a second and final hint, such as: "It's the alcohol you had that night when you ran into the supermarket and got arrested for indecent use of a zucchini."

Scoring

100 points if the player guesses the correct answer immediately after the first drink, with his teammate giving no hint.

75 points if the player names the correct alcohol after the second drink and his teammate has given only one hint.

50 points if the player takes the third drink and needs a second hint to answer correctly.

If the player is not able to guess the drink correctly at all, the team gets an unopened box of pencils—no points. Ha!

After the team has correctly identified the alcohol or when they've exhausted their guesses, they get one more opportunity to score.

The blindfolded person will throw a ping-pong ball to their teammate, who may stand anywhere he wants so long as it's at least fifteen feet from his blindfolded partner. The catcher must shout out, "Run, run, Marla Runyan!" to help his blind partner know where to throw the ball. He may not say anything else.

If the blindfolded player makes the catch, the team earns fifty points.

Two more rounds follow in the same way. After each round alternate which teammate drinks.

Suggested shots for beginners: tequila, whiskey, bourbon, gin, vodka, Jägermeister, and rum.

Shots for experts: get different brands of each spirit. For instance, get five brands of vodka, and then the blind contestant must not only

correctly identify that it is vodka but also must guess the exact brand.

At the end of the match each player must drunk-dial his grandma.

You: Grandma! Did you know there was a *blind* Olympian?! Oh, and the reason I'm banned from the supermarket is because I fondled a zucchini.

Your grandma: That's great!

You: Did you hear what I said?

Your grandma: Yes, you have a blind date with a zucchini.

You: Turn on your hearing aid!

Your grandma: You kids today do it differently, but love is love. I hope you two make a very happy salad.

You: Grandma, are you off your medication?

Your grandma: I have to go, sweetheart. My friends and I at the senior living facility are in the middle of the Misty Hyman drinking game! Misty Hyman—what a name! Ha!

DRINKING
QUIZ

What Kind of
Drunk Are You?

When you're drunk, which are you most likely to do?

Do you

drool, spit when you talk, vomit on yourself or others, and attempt to perform moves from the Brazilian martial arts dance of capoeira in the bar and wind up slipping in your own drool and vomit then leaping up with puke on the left side of your face and announce, "I'm okay, folks! That was *cap-where-ah!* Now, *where-ah* my ladies at?! Whoop whoop!"

If so, you are a . . .

Sloppy drunk

Or do you

crack jokes, smile, and be generous? If your car gets towed, you shout out, "Cool! I get to visit the impound later! I'll cheer up the mustachioed lady at the desk with my charm! Mustachioed kinda sounds like pistachioed! Hey, I'd rather kiss a girl with a hairy lip than a woman with salty nuts! Am I right? Who's giving out high fives? *This* guy!"

That makes you a . . .

Happy drunk

Or do you

shout out in the middle of the crowded bar: "I discovered my girl-friend's dirty secret! I found a twisted horn hidden in her underwear drawer! And handcuffs! Oh my God! She's a unicorn hunter!"

You are definitely an . . .

Inappropriate drunk

Or do you

go up to a good-looking person and begin rambling, "Esss, q's eeee. I'd like to make a toast. Isn't that a stupid phrase? I want a *drink*, not *breakfast* . . . unless it's with you tomorrow morning. I hope you don't have morning breath. Speaking of harsh breath, did you know that in Western mythology dragons are evil fire-breathers, but in Eastern lore dragons are good heavenly creatures? What both cultures *can* agree on is that unicorns are gay. I can imagine an offended unicorn protesting, 'I'm not gay! I'm a mighty horny horse!' A beautiful panther is called a leopard, but when a horse is *fabulous* you call him gay!"

You are the . . .

Talkative drunk

Or do you,

at a house party, accidentally step on a cat's tail, stumble over to the host to apologize, and in the process knock over someone's white Russian and a sentimental-looking vase that some jerk must've used to put out cigarettes because ashes pour all over the floor and into the spilled drink that the cat begins to lick up? The host then screams something about her beloved mamaw and drops to her knees to clean the mess. You bend over to help but fall off balance, and when you lift your head your face has a cool looking five o'clock shadow.

You are the . . .

Falling-down drunk

Or are you

likely to announce to everyone: "Ohhh, I ate too much at the Mexican restaurant. Now I'm pregnant with a baby. Her name is Fajita Sam Plar"? Then you continue to whoever will listen: "Get it? Eh? Eh? Pull my finger. I'm going to make a toilet burrito so big I'll need to break it up with a stick like a piñata!"

You are the . . .

Annoying drunk

Or do you

adopt a calm demeanor and deliberate philosophically, "I'm having second thoughts about my second thoughts. Does that make them fourth thoughts? I think I think too much. Bah! I did it again!"

You are the . . .

Cerebral drunk

Or do you

cry out, "I love you, maaaaammal! You're the best doggy! Come here, you furry ball of warmth! From now on when you go on walks, I won't get short tempered when you stop to sniff stuff. In fact, I'll sniff it with you! We need to bond! I want to know what's so interesting about that patch of grass by the Fernandez house!"

You are obviously the . . .

Emotional drunk

Or do you

have an alcohol-soaked epiphany and say, "Bedbugs live in beds. Grasshoppers live in the grass. So how did cockroaches get named? *Aaaahhh!*"

You are the . . .

Dumb drunk

Even though we're all *different kinds* of drunk, we are *equal* under the eye of alcohol. You will see that the first letter of each type of drunk spells out what unites us! We are all . . . *Shitfaced.*

Summer Olympic Games Host Cities

1896—Athens, Greece

1900—Paris, France

1904—St. Louis, United States

1908—London, England

1912—Stockholm, Sweden

1920—Antwerp, Belgium

1924—Paris, France

1928—Amsterdam, Netherlands

1932—Los Angeles, United States

1936—Berlin, Germany

1948—London, England

1952—Helsinki, Finland

1956—Melbourne, Australia

1960—Rome, Italy

1964—Tokyo, Japan

1968—Mexico City, Mexico

1972—Munich, Germany

1976—Montreal, Canada

1980—Moscow, USSR

1984—Los Angeles, United States

1988—Seoul, South Korea

1992—Barcelona, Spain

1996—Atlanta, United States

2000—Sydney, Australia

2004—Athens, Greece

2008—Beijing, China

2012—London, England

Winter Olympic Games Host Cities

1924—Chamonix, France

1928—St. Moritz, Switzerland

1932—Lake Placid, United States

1936—Garmisch-Partenkirchen, Germany

1948—St. Moritz, Switzerland

1952—Oslo, Norway

1956—Cortina d'Ampezzo, Italy

1960—Squaw Valley, United States

1964—Innsbruck, Austria

1968—Grenoble, France

1972—Sapporo, Japan

1976—Innsbruck, Austria

1980—Lake Placid, United States

1984—Sarajevo, Yugoslavia

1988—Calgary, Alberta, Canada

1992—Albertville, France

1994—Lillehammer, Norway

1998—Nagano, Japan

2002—Salt Lake City, United States

2006—Turin, Italy

2010—Vancouver, Canada

2014—Sochi, Russia

Acknowledgments

I would like to thank the fine people who made this book possible. Thank you, Jordana Tusman, editor extraordinaire, for your hard work. Thank you, good people at Running Press and Perseus Books Group. Thank you, Holly Schmidt and Allan Penn at Hollan Publishing for putting this deal together.

As a youngster, my sense of humor was forever molded by a number of unique voices, some of whom I'd like to specifically thank at this time. Howard Stern taught me to push boundaries, be myself, and feel free to goof on anything. I've always admired his hysterical creativity. Al Lowe, creator of the *Leisure Suit Larry* video games, warped my mind in the best possible way. I spent a good portion of my childhood with his hilarious and clever games. I loved the outrageous silliness of Adam Sandler's albums. *MAD* magazine made me giggle uncontrollably for years, and it was an incredible honor when they published my work.

I'd also like to thank three of my fellow comedians who have also been great friends, Maddog Mattern, Ruhbin Mehta, and Neil Charles. I've made a lot of good friends while performing, and these guys have been particularly supportive and inspirational—and funny too! Check them out!

The games and stories in this book were read by some very good people who were like comedy Beta Testers. Thank you, Alison Reilly Fox, Carole Prikasky, Christina Wright Riseman, Luba Bogopolskaya, Michael Schechter, Nicollete Bernardino, and Stevie Curry. And an extraspecial thank you to Paul Dean, Paulina Leoniak, and Evan Lieberman for their detailed feedback and support.

Thank you, Scott Kaar, Ian Langsam, and Ron Mallick for your encouragement.

Finally, thank you to Judy and Larry, my parents. They are like two love birds—if love birds screeched like hawks intimidating their prey. They have been a source of extraordinarily great material through the years. And they're pretty cool people too. If you're out there playing my drinking games, be sure to invite my parents. My dad will happily play along and get wasted. My mom won't drink, but she will be a cheerleader for my dad. And by cheerleader, I mean she'll be jumping up and down yelling, "Stop drinking, you moron! Let's go home!"

The End